YOU DON'T HAVE TO BE

FAMOUS

HOW TO WRITE YOUR LIFE STORY

STEVE ZOUSMER

WRITER'S DIGEST BOOKS
Cincinnati, Ohio
www.writersdigest.com

APR   2010

Distributed in Canada by Fraser Direct, 100 Armstrong Avenue, Georgetown, ON, Canada L7G 5S4, Tel: (905) 877-4411. Distributed in the UK and Europe by David & Charles, Brunel House, Newton Abbot, Devon, TQ12 4PU, England, Tel: (+44) 1626 323200, Fax: (+44) 1626 323319, E-mail: postmaster@davidandcharles.co.uk. Distributed in Australia by Capricorn Link, P.O. Box 704, Windsor, NSW 2756 Australia, Tel: (02) 4577-3555.

Visit our Web site at www.writersdigest.com and www.wdeditors.com for information on more resources for writers.

To receive a free weekly e-mail newsletter delivering tips and updates about writing and about Writer's Digest products, register directly at our Web site at http://newsletters.fwpublications.com.

11 10 09 08 07   5 4 3 2 1

Library of Congress Cataloging-in-Publication Data

Zousmer, Steve.

  You don't have to be famous : how to write your life story / by Steve Zousmer.

      p. cm.

  ISBN 978-1-58297-439-2 (hardcover. : alk. paper)

  ISBN 978-1-58297-438-5 (pbk. : alk. paper)

  1. Autobiography--Authorship. I. Title.

  CT25.Z68 2007

  808'.06692--dc22   2007001521

Edited by Michelle Ehrhard

Designed by Eric West

Production coordinated by Mark Griffin

ABOUT THE AUTHOR

Steve Zousmer has had a highly diversified career as a writer. He started out as a newspaper reporter in Providence, RI, and San Francisco, and later worked as a writer and producer at ABC News, where he was chief writer of *Good Morning America* and a senior producer of *Nightline*. He wrote documentary films for National Geographic, the Smithsonian, the Audubon Society, and Discovery. He has written for magazines and the op-ed pages of the *New York Times*, *Washington Post* and *Wall Street Journal*. For seventeen years he has been a speechwriter for the CEOs and presidents of more than thirty major companies. He has taught writing at five large corporations and at the Columbia University Graduate School of Journalism. This is his fifth book.

He lives in a New York suburb with his wife and two children.

DEDICATION

This one's for Gracie.

TABLE OF CONTENTS

───── ✸ ─────

FOREWORD

Winston Churchill said, "I like to learn, but I don't like to be taught." I feel the same way. I have the greatest respect for teachers (and I've taught several hundred students in writing courses at five major companies), but I will not be acting like a teacher in this book. I will not ask you to do drills or exercises or take quizzes at the end of chapters—largely because I don't like books that make you do drills or exercises or take quizzes.

I will not urge you to admire a lot of writing examples by big-name writers. I've always felt that writing examples are overrated because a student sees only the polished, final product rather than the steps and missteps of construction; *that* would be instructive—showing the decisions and improvements the writer made while struggling toward the finished product.

I will not promise magic solutions in the form of five-easy-steps formulas for writing success. I dislike books that promise an easy way because there is no easy way. The difficulty of writing is proof that formulas don't work. Your book will be an achievement to be proud of *because* writing is difficult. Frankly, even if formulas worked, you wouldn't want a one-size-fits-all or off-the-rack solution for your life story. It's too unique and important for that. Other than a rudimentary, structural outline, there is no paint-by-the-numbers template for a good creative work.

There are endless ways to write and structure your autobiography. It's your book, and you should enjoy and embrace your almost unlimited freedom to write it any way you want and for whatever purpose you choose. You can devise your own approach or select from several traditional models, which I'll describe. I'll try to help you focus on your aspirations for your book and make the best decisions about how to write it.

The fact that you're holding this book in your hands indicates that you want to write your book on your own, without a traditional teacher or classroom environment, either because you're disinclined to bring others into your process or because you want to shortcut the learning process and get down to business quickly.

My approach is *not* geared for creative writing students or anyone trying to build a foundation for long-term growth as a writer. My goal is to help you accomplish one fine thing and one thing only: writing your autobiography.

While most of my advice is familiar to anyone who's studied writing, some of it is expedient and against the grain of campus writing mantra. Creative writing teachers might be slightly appalled.

My suggestion is that you digest this whole book before beginning your autobiography. If you are bursting with start-up energy and don't want to wait that long, read at least through chapter ten—and then keep reading as you write. But you'll be better off if you finish the reading before you begin the writing.

Keep in mind that the longer and more ambitious your book is going to be, the more painfully early mistakes or a bad start will catch up with you. Somewhere around page 20 or 40 or 60, you'll realize that cracks are spreading rapidly through the foundation. The only thing to do is to go back and figure out what you've done wrong and make the needed repairs. This could mean a lot of work; it might even mean junking everything and starting over from scratch.

We don't want this to happen because it could knock the wind out of your enthusiasm, jeopardizing the whole project. Writing requires momentum and fortitude and losing both at an early stage does not bode well. You might put your manuscript in a drawer—out of sight because you can't bear to even look at it. Two years later, you'll throw it out.

Countless writing projects have met this fate. I think it happens largely because inexperienced writers don't think about the big stuff—they are too preoccupied with relatively small stuff, such as technique. They want to start driving nails and erecting walls and chimneys without thinking enough about the blueprint of their house and what kind of house it will be and *why* they are building it. Nail-driving skills will get them only so far if they have no answers when they encounter the big questions.

So I want to prepare you to start well—by which I mean not just writing a few good opening pages but going in with something better than a beginner's concept of what the book-writing marathon is all about. *If you don't start well you probably won't finish*, and autobiography will be just another of those quickly abandoned hobbies you'd prefer to forget. This is why I'm asking you to keep reading until I've given you as much help as I possibly can. As of this moment, the foremost writing hazard facing you is an impetuous start.

If my years as a writer have taught me two things, one is about the importance of the *right* start (because it's the first step in creating a structure, because you have fresh energy that'll never come again, and because it's a big, ice-breaking step emotionally), and the other is about something that comes largely *before* the start—developing a clear understanding of your motivation and the *purpose* of what you are writing.

These two topics, starting and motivation, will get what might seem to be disproportionate attention in this book, and you might find yourself wondering when I'm going to get around to nitty-gritty writing advice. So I think it might help if I give you a thumbnail description of how this book is organized.

In chapter one, I'll make the case for something I consider essential to your success in writing your auto-biography: You have to swear off all fantasies of literary fame and fortune and focus on writing a "private" autobiography, meaning a book for a limited audience of family and friends.

Chapter two will answer basic questions that people always ask about the process of book writing. Chapter three digs into the importance of determining your motivation for writing your life story. Most people structure their autobiographies chronologically but there are other good options, so in chapter four, we'll work on choosing an organizing principle.

In chapter five, we'll talk about research and outlining, and you might be surprised by my warning to go light on both. Chapter six is about the challenge of developing your primary writing instrument—your "voice"—and matching it to your audience. Chapter seven confronts an intimidating central issue—writing is hard—and offers advice on defeating writer's block and dealing with the various emotional stresses that complicate writing.

Chapter eight is about embracing the creativity of writing, allowing your imagination to be free and audacious—operating under the wide latitude of what I call "The Waiver," but never violating the requirement to tell the truth. In chapter nine, we'll look at strategies for getting over the hurdle of starting—whether you're starting the book, a chapter, a section, or a story.

Because stories will figure so prominently in your autobiography, we'll spend chapter ten talking about recognizing, selecting, and telling your best stories. Chapter eleven provides general writing advice that will help you raise the level of your game as you get deeper into your book.

Then in chapter twelve, we'll cover a special area that will be of great significance to some writers but a minimal concern for others (depending on how revealingly they choose to discuss their lives): how to deal with the sensitive matter of writing about people close to you and things to consider as you handle the negative events of a lifetime, the "things we don't talk about."

From that point, we'll turn into the homestretch, discussing the all-important skill of rewriting in chapter thirteen. Then, in chapter fourteen, we'll look at the postwriting experience—bracing yourself for reader reactions, deciding how to distribute or self-publish the book, and your option to add audio and video supplements as part of a multimedia approach to autobiography. (In the appendix, I'll discuss writing and producing a video profile of yourself.)

★ ★ ★

Since we're going to spend the next few hundred pages together, I should tell you a bit about my background as a writer.

I grew up in a writing environment. Both my parents were journalists, as were most of the visitors to our house. My high school girlfriend's father and grandfather were the science editors of the Associated Press; she became a science writer herself and has written at least one best-selling nonfiction book. I met my wife in a TV news-room and most of *our* friends have come from journalism or other fields of communication.

In addition to writing help from my parents, I had memorable English teachers in high school. As an under-graduate, I was in the great Stanford University creative writing program taught by Wallace Stegner and Richard Scowcroft. As a graduate student in journalism at Columbia University, I had still more excellent writing teachers, and then I went out in the real world and had numerous good editors who continued my education.

I was a reporter for two newspapers; a Navy information officer and speechwriter for six admirals; a TV news writer and producer at ABC News; a documentary film-writer (National Geographic/Smithsonian/Audubon/Discovery); and, for many years, a speechwriter for the CEOs and presidents of more than thirty big corporations.

I have written op-eds and magazine pieces and five books, including one about broadcast writing, one about speech writing, and now this one about autobiography writing.

The book I have not written is my own autobiography, but I'm hoping it will be my next big project. I'll discuss my current thinking on it at the end of this book in the after-word, "My Not-Yet-Written Autobiography."

1

YOU DON'T HAVE
TO BE FAMOUS

You should do it.

Write your life story.

This might be a new idea to you or something you've thought about for years. Either way, for any of many good reasons, the time might now be right.

It is an ambitious undertaking, an exciting possibility. But if you're like most people, your enthusiasm is tempered by a wave of doubts.

You're thinking: Autobiographies are written by famous people, and I'm not one of them. When I browse the autobiography section of bookstores, I do not see books written by unfamous people like me. Isn't this a clue that I am not a member of the club of potential autobiographers? And to be blunt, when I compare myself to published autobiographers, what in the world makes me think I am *worthy* of a book? My life isn't really that interesting. I don't have that much to say. I'm not a writer, but I've done enough writing to know that writing is hard. I could never write a book. Even if I *could* write a book, no one would buy it.

These are common first reactions to the idea of writing an autobiography. It's impossible to know how many autobiography projects never got off the ground because of them. Or how many how-to books about writing autobiography were briefly glanced through but then hurriedly put back on bookstore shelves because people are so quick to disqualify themselves. Or how many wonderful life stories have not been preserved, and how many families and friends who would have treasured those stories have been left, instead, with nothing.

The number must be very big. But I also know that unfamous people *have* been writing their autobiographies quietly and successfully for decades, for centuries, and they are doing it *now* in unprecedented numbers. They are taking classes, joining autobiography clubs, reading how-to books, or working on their own in classic writer solitude.

Like you, they feel a pull to write their life story. They recognize that it's something they want to do or need to do, something they would find enjoyable and enriching, something with long-lasting value. They're right. But they're also right to consider the doubts I've mentioned because these doubts are not insignificant.

Like most things that are really worth doing, writing an autobiography is a formidable challenge, and the odds are against you if you dash in wide-eyed and unprepared. I don't want you to pour a lot of time, energy, emotion, and good intentions into writing anything except *the book that's right for you*, because trying to write the *wrong* book for the *wrong* reasons will lead you precisely to the out-

YOU DON'T HAVE TO BE FAMOUS

come that would-be writers correctly dread: fast, frustrating, painful and embarrassing defeat.

This is regrettable and avoidable and shouldn't happen, yet it happens constantly. A high percentage of writing projects are doomed before the first words are written because the writer goes in with objectives that range from nonexistent to unlikely to impossible. The sad part is that such a small amount of clarity or good advice would have chased away those wrong notions and put the writer on a course for success.

So let's begin by looking closely at your doubts and seeing how, on examination, each apparent limitation helps define a solution that makes your goal realistically achievable.

FORGET ABOUT FAME AND FORTUNE

Aspiring autobiographers complicate their prospects with two notions regarding fame and fortune. The first is that they'll never be published because they're not famous. The second is that they will somehow be published *anyway*, and will then rocket to glory.

I'll always remember a scene from the TV sitcom *Cheers* in which the hilariously rude waitress Carla smacks a dithering customer with her dishtowel and barks at him, "Get on the train to reality." Getting on the train to reality is healthy, invigorating, and even empowering, and I'm hoping you will jump aboard, starting by getting all fame-and-fortune thinking out of your head. The first step is to banish the fantasy that you are going to be discovered and make headlines as an author.

**Local Man's Autobiography Is Best-Seller:
Signs Mega-Bucks Movie Deal**

School Nurse's Story Wins Nobel Prize:
Will Guest on Oprah

These seductive fantasies flicker in the minds of all writers. But the reality is that your story is not suited for the prime time of national publication. While it happens on rare occasions that an unknown writer produces a successful novel or thriller and reaps a highly publicized bonanza, an autobiography by an unknown and inexperienced writer has virtually no appeal to publishers.

So your concern that you'll never be signed to a publishing deal because you're not famous is at least 99 percent accurate, probably higher. Your name has no brand recognition. You have no "author platform" (meaning unique qualities that might attract attention or add appeal to your book). Your story, while possibly very good, is not compelling *enough* to differentiate it from other stories—if it *were* that compelling, you would probably have attracted a certain amount of notice, even fame, and you'd have a chance.

But for most of us, that hasn't happened and will not happen. So we would be rejected by publishers for the most clear-cut and fatal of reasons: Our autobiographies are *not marketable*.

Being unmarketable is an economic reality but not a character defect. Nor is it a character defect of publishers to insist on an affirmative answer to "Can this book *sell?*" Some publishers, such as university presses or small specialty houses, have different viewpoints and might be less profit-minded, but there is always a financial context.

I think we have to concede that this makes sense. If you were a publisher, you would probably *not* be willing to invest company money underwriting the publication of *Mildred Seplavy: I Did It My Way.* As a shopper in a book-

YOU DON'T HAVE TO BE FAMOUS

store, you would not shell out $17.95 for a copy of Leo Femish's *My Fifty Years in Dry Cleaning*.

The consequences of unmarketability are so obvious, they are not even worthy of Economics 101, yet we who write are fragile dreamers and deniers of reality, always clinging to hopes of rainbows and pots of gold and a taste of public adulation. But we have to let go of this fantasy; it will only get in the way.

Right now, you may be nodding in reluctant agreement, but a little voice inside you is protesting, "Okay, I'll play this game and pretend to accept that I'm unmarketable. But I'll show 'em. I'll be the exception. My book will be so special, it'll be the one that breaks through the marketability barrier."

But you're kidding yourself, and I'm not going to encourage you to keep dreaming because the serious point here is that living with this illusion is *not* harmless. You are embracing the *wrong* ambition. It will confuse your motivation, point you in wrong directions, influence every sentence you write, and drastically reduce your chances of finishing. You'll try to write the wrong book, and you won't get far.

Book writing is a hard enough; you don't need a huge, fundamental mistake before you even begin. You would be so much better off if you would conduct open-heart surgery on yourself right now, removing every vestige of yearning for fame and fortune and implanting instead the single *right* ambition: to write a good book, with no reward other than that.

Therefore, the book I want to persuade you to write is *not* a book you're going to sell. You're going to give it away *free*. Instead of aiming for a wide, commercial audience you'll never reach, I'm urging you to write a *private autobiography*, by which I mean a book for a limited audience composed of the people you care about most: your spouse, your kids, your grandchildren, your friends, or just yourself. Or some combination thereof.

You will print it out or self-publish it in some simple form (there are many ways to do this—see chapter fourteen), and it will be the best gift you ever gave. You will put your heart into it, pour your thoughts and memories into it, and make it something that's uniquely you and will last forever.

Later in this chapter, I'll describe writing advantages you'll enjoy as an unfamous writer. But for now, the point is: *You'll write a better book because you're not famous.*

DON'T THINK THAT YOU'RE UNINTERESTING

Now let's move on to another of your doubts, the one about not being interesting enough. It is true that you might not be interesting to a wide audience of people who've never heard of you, but you *are* interesting to a small and carefully selected private audience of family and friends. You've lived your life among them and shared your life with them. You are probably a central figure in their lives, and they are central to yours—they will probably appear in many of the scenes you'll describe. This audience will be *very* interested in you.

As for your doubt about not having that much to say, I guarantee that this worry will dissolve as you begin to tap into the autobiography process. In his poem "Song of Myself," Walt Whitman wrote, "I am large. I contain multitudes," and this turns out to be true of all of us. I'm presuming that most would-be autobiographers are over fifty,

YOU DON'T HAVE TO BE FAMOUS

which means you have fifty or more *years* of memories. Even if you're only twenty-five, that's a quarter century of life experience to draw on. Rather than having nothing to say, you will find that your biggest problem will be controlling an avalanche of memories and material.

But of course *quantity* of memories isn't the issue, and I will bet that as you examine your life, you'll discover many memories with story *quality* equal to the stories of the most celebrated autobiographers. It's all there, it's just a matter of training yourself to recognize your best stories and retrieve them from memory.

We'll talk later about how to do this. But for now, the point is that *you have good stories to tell*, and the only difference between you and members of the fame club is that their stories are on a grander and usually public scale. Alexander the Great conquered the world, and you might not be able to make that same claim, but you've had battles, triumphs, and tragedies, too, and the only question is whether you can make them as interesting, or more interesting, than Alexander's. And for your private audience, you *can*. So don't dismiss your life as uninteresting because it's not earthshaking—most of the people who've shaken the earth are forgotten fairly swiftly, anyway, and their memories are not cherished as your family will cherish yours.

YOU ARE WORTHY

This connects directly to another doubt, the one about your *worth* as the subject of an autobiography. Let's come right out and admit that you have not conquered the world; you've never even been president of a major nation. You have never cured a disease, starred in a blockbuster movie, or performed as a prima ballerina or a Super Bowl quarterback. Does this mean that you are an insignificant toad, that your existence has had no importance to your spouse or children or parents or friends or others whose lives you've touched? No, to them your story is important. There is no question that your story is worth telling; the question is whether you can do justice to telling it.

But you have doubts about that. "I'm not a writer," you say. "I could never write a book."

Good. Acknowledging that you are *not* a writer is far more positive than pretending you are one or hoping you will magically turn into one. It is a strange thing about writing that while people have no problem with the idea that they could never become an opera star or a brain surgeon, they think that *if they really tried,* they could become fine writers. Then they try it, and it's like crashing into a brick wall.

So here's a second harsh reality to go with the reality about not getting your book published or becoming rich and famous: Unless you are a professional writer, you will not write a professional-quality autobiography. But you can write a high-quality *amateur* autobiography.

I don't mean *amateurish*—I mean amateur in the original sense (derived from the Latin word meaning lover): one who may be as competent as a professional but is motivated by a love or passion for the activity, one who engages in a pursuit as a pastime rather than as a profession.

Love and passion are not always part of the professional's tool kit, but they can be part of yours. Combine them with good preparation, good decisions, and your unequalled knowledge of your own life, and you'll be equipped to write something that might be far more desirable and unique than a professionally written book.

I will help you find your writing voice, select anecdotes and approaches that bring your story to life, and write honestly, interestingly, and, if you wish, bravely. Instead of being a professional writing for a large, faceless audience, you will be *you* telling your stories directly to people you know very well. You can collapse the usual distance between writer and reader and bring to bear all of the powers of writing in what amounts to something close to a face-to-face conversation (in which you do all the talking).

Will this be easy? Not a chance. But I'm presuming that if you've picked up this book with some interest in writing your autobiography, you are not intimidated—at least not *prohibitively* intimidated—by the challenge of writing a book.

This is important. You may have done a lot of writing and might be a good writer already, and of course this helps, too, although you may have to unlearn or alter your present writing style to deal with the first-person voice and relatively intimate narrative style of autobiography. This is not, for example, the way doctors, lawyers, academics, or business executives usually write. If you've spent many years in a bureaucracy, you will probably have to undergo a style-ectomy to prepare yourself for autobiography.

But whether you've done a lot of writing or relatively little, you probably will not be surprised by the idea that *writing is hard*. I find it distressing when how-to-write authors suggest that writing will be a breeze—just follow their instructions, and everything will be fine. I've never met a writer who would say that writing is easy, yet these how-to authors seem to think that if they tell you the truth, you will panic and run for the exits. My view, on the other hand, is that if you realize it's going to be hard, you *won't* panic when you run into the inevitable difficulties. And you won't say, "Oh, if this is so easy for everyone else but so hard for me, it must mean that I'm just not cut out for this, so I quit."

Writing was hard for the immortals, and it will be hard for you. And it won't be less hard because you are an amateur writing for an audience of family and friends. Writing is an equal-opportunity tormentor.

If you've never written a book, I don't see how you could *not* have doubts about your ability to do so. But I am telling you that the doubts and difficulties can be overcome. What's important is to see trouble coming so you're not paralyzed when it strikes, so you understand the predictable problems that afflict every writer, and so you know what to do to survive and keep writing. Throughout this book, I'll try to prepare you for the difficulties and help you surmount them. But be ready for a wrestling match.

And be ready to wrestle *alone*. Writing is a solitary pursuit. Many writers are gregarious social creatures, but when the time comes, they can flip a switch and turn from party animals into lonely monks slaving away in cloistered cells. Some people are not built for this isolation and solitude, even for just a few hours at a time. Silence unnerves them. They require company and group support.

I mention this as a caution, and I'll talk briefly about ways to bring other people into the process (classes, clubs, writing partners, and hiring editors to work with you). But ultimately there is no getting around the reality that writing is done solo, not socially.

And yet, in a different sense, you are *not* alone. There is a great heritage you can draw on for support, a brotherhood and a sisterhood of writers who've been at this

YOU DON'T HAVE TO BE FAMOUS

for thousands of years, who've faced the same large and small writing problems you will face, and have battled through to solutions.

Writers who've come before you have discovered eternal truths that guide writing success as well as tricks of the trade that make the process less torturous. Others have learned from good teachers and editors and other writers and from countless hours of pounding it out, throwing it away, cursing and swearing, quitting and returning, finally getting it right. All of this adds up to a body of knowledge that reduces isolation and provides guidance and advice, encouragement, useful instruction and pointers, references, anecdotes, larger context, even moral support and spirit-raising. My job is to be your link to this heritage. Writing your book might be one of the best experiences of your life, and I am determined to help you do it.

ADVANTAGES OF PRIVATE AUTOBIOGRAPHY

It's not that you give up ambitions for literary fame and fortune without getting something in return. I think there are a number of valuable advantages for an unfamous author writing a private autobiography.

You have the freedom to create the book that is just right for you and just right for your chosen private audience. You don't have to fit it into anyone else's structure or format.

You will have total creative ownership and freedom, constrained only by honesty and common sense.

You will have the pure writing experience, as uncontaminated as possible by ego and the profit motive.

You will feel no pressure to dramatize, distort, or hype anything in your life to make the book a more marketable read—indeed, marketability disappears as a factor (though *readability* does not disappear as a goal).

You will have total liberty to include *or exclude* sensitive and extremely personal details and episodes of your life. In a nationally published book, you would not get away with sidestepping such areas, which would be considered the indispensable "juicy parts" you would be expected to deal with in detail.

Levels of candor and disclosure will be completely up to you. Once you've found your comfort levels, difficult decisions will be much easier, as if you had a *policy* to guide you in dealing with these issues rather than facing a new crisis every time sensitive matters come up.

The depth of digging into your interior life will be under your control. You can go deep or stay near the surface. Because of your limited and friendly audience, you might be more open and candid and less formal or self-conscious than you would be before a wider audience—and perhaps less prone to self-justification or defensiveness.

To whatever degree you like, you will be able to probe in memory and reflection to *discover* things about your life. You will be able to go off in spontaneous or unorthodox directions, perhaps retrieving little diamonds of memory, which, like an old locket or some forgotten souvenir, awaken emotions that register powerfully with you or your family even if they would seem too trivial to mention before a wider audience. Finding new layers of meaning is one of the great attractions of writing autobiography, and it's an area in which a private autobiography has the potential to be superior to autobiographies by famous people.

I've noted that many (though not all) famous autobiographers stick to the outward script of their lives with minimal introspection and discovery. They don't seem too interested in digging to new layers, maybe because their purpose is more about marketability than meanings, and their readers are presumed to be content with the story on the surface. A few backstage barbs or confessional tidbits are enough to make readers think they're getting a peek behind the curtain.

Discovery is even more unlikely when a ghostwriter or as-told-to writer is doing the writing. With some autobiographies—notably by sports stars and celebrities—it seems that hired writers have assembled the book from newspaper and magazine clippings, possibly without making the acquaintance of the so-called "author." The retired basketball star Charles Barkley made a mockery of the sports autobiography genre when he complained of being misquoted in his own autobiography.

Writing a private autobiography will also give you an advantage in terms of a challenge that can become a terminally difficult obstacle for inexperienced writers: finding your writing voice. "Voice" means not only the language you use but the character and personality you present in print. I'll discuss it at length later on, but the upside is that voice will probably come easier to you because you are addressing your wife or husband, your son or granddaughter, or your best friends. You know them, and they know you, which means you might be able to find a comfortable voice (or wavelength) faster than you would with an audience of strangers.

One final benefit of writing your own privately circulated book is that it will not be sent out into the cold, cruel world. You won't have to deal with painful rejections by agents and publishers; you won't have to struggle to market your book; you won't have the unsettling experience of coping with weird or hostile reactions by strangers; and you won't be vulnerable to reviews of your book by people with the power to make extremely hurtful judgments on you.

The only judgments will come from people who already love you.

Advantages of Being an Amateur

Repeat after me: *I will never write as well as Philip Roth or Toni Morrison or John Updike or Joan Didion. Nor will I ever approach a fraction of their critical and financial success.*

Be content with being yourself, working within your limitations, not trying to hit notes beyond your range but seizing these advantages of being an amateur:

- Writing from the heart, in plain language, more than compensates for lack of craft, skill, or stylistic sophistication.

- You have an enormous home-court advantage because you know the subject (your life) better than anyone.

- The emotional connection and historical context with your readers already exists and does not need to be imagined and skillfully constructed.

- If you do not pretend to professional quality, you will not be judged (harshly) by professional standards. If you make a serious effort, it will be respected, and the result will be admired and envied.

As long as you're content with the reality of being an amateur doing what you can do—not wasting effort and emotion doing what you can't do—the conditions are ideal for your success.

"NEW AUTOBIOGRAPHY"

You should be aware of a current movement called New Autobiography, which has apparently created a surge of excitement about autobiography writing, with people joining "memoir clubs" and taking autobiography classes.

I hesitate to generalize about New Autobiography, and I'm not even sure I can describe it fairly, but the main idea seems to be about mixing fictional techniques with memoir to create something richer and deeper than the straightforward, summary-style, traditional autobiography.

The primary techniques to be borrowed from fiction involve the invention of dialogue and the construction of dramatic scenes that might have or could have taken place, or *would have* taken place if reality obeyed the requirements of literature. But instead of presenting these conversations and scenes as autobiographical fiction, they are considered permissible as nonfiction *embellished* by a creative writing imagination.

This is where it gets tricky. Poetic or artistic license has always been acceptable for writers and artists because everyone understands the rules they're playing by. Gustave Flaubert would alter a fact because he disliked its impact on his beautifully cadenced sentences; James McNeill Whistler would paint your portrait, but if he thought your brown eyes clashed with the composition, you got blue eyes (unless you were Whistler's mother).

But what happens when license to alter facts is extended to writers in a nonfiction genre like autobiography? It's not clear what limits New Autobiography writers observe in stretching known reality for dramatic or literary affect, but their goal *is* clear: a memoir that reads like fiction but is presumably more insightful than a nonfiction narrative, which is limited to actual, provable, literal truth. Poetic truth is regarded as *superior* truth, even if it takes liberties with the what-really-happened truth.

While people of all ages are working away at New Autobiography, it seems to be mostly about youngish people who aspire not only to illumination and creative fulfillment but also to literary recognition and perhaps financial success. This, of course, is quite different from the private and amateur book I've been prescribing as your approach to autobiography. If you want to know more about it, the best book I've found is *Your Life as Story: Discovering the "New Autobiography" and Writing Memoir as Literature* by Tristine Rainer.

Ms. Rainer is a teacher, and probably an excellent one, if you are attracted to a "memoir as literature" approach. She describes New Autobiography using the word *experiential*, and, while I distrust trendy and nebulous language of that sort, I get the idea that New Autobiography gives the experience of the *writer* a higher priority than the book's value to the *reader*. This clashes with my humble priority of leaving an earnest account of your life for family, friends, and generations yet unborn.

What I've been suggesting (and I'm not finished) is that big choices have to be made as you embark on

YOU DON'T HAVE TO BE FAMOUS

writing your autobiography. The New Autobiography approach might be more to your liking than a traditional approach. Deep down, I'm not convinced that New Autobiography is necessarily *that* different from the traditional approach, though it's clearly different in motivation.

I'm very much in favor of digging for meaning and believe writers should do that, when they can. I'm not against opinion, interpretation, or even speculation *as long as they are openly labeled as such* and not confused with verifiable truth. I'm not against "poetic" or "artistic" truth as long as the writer can make a convincing case for it and distinguishes between what is certain and what is imagined. As for inventing dialogue or details out of thin air, I get uncomfortable with this the moment it goes beyond a sentence or two of simple scene setting or paraphrasing and moves into significant re-invention of history.

Generally I would prefer the authenticity of the true story with its holes and flaws clearly acknowledged, even if the final result is dramatically incomplete and acknowledges that key questions remain unanswered: "While I recall that conversation clearly, I have no memory of what happened afterwards." "I don't know what caused Jane to move to Minnesota, but this incident was probably a factor."

My reservations about New Autobiography undoubtedly reflect my journalistic background. Journalists are taught that embellishing or imagining the truth to even the smallest degree is strictly out of bounds because readers don't know what's true and what's imagined and also because it compromises the writer's credibility. So if credibility is important in your autobiography, compromising it jumps out as an ill-advised negative.

As an example of an autobiography that finds a brilliant middle ground between disciplined reporting and crossing the line into poetic license, I highly recommend Geoffrey Wolff's book, *The Duke of Deception: Memories of My Father*. This is the rare autobiography in which the focus is not on the autobiographer. Wolff describes his memories of his father, the "Duke," a devoted parent but also a frighteningly troubled con man and scam artist who dragged his wife and sons through agonizing adventures that Wolff remembers vividly and sensitively. I had unquestioning respect for Wolff's credibility and no suspicion that he was embellishing or using the truth as raw material for fiction. (It should be noted that Wolff is also a gifted fiction writer and author of six novels.)

The Duke of Deception supports my view that it's not necessary to make an either/or choice between the objective nonfiction- and fiction-writing models. I think your own preferences will evolve quickly as you get into telling your story.

There is much more to be said about autobiography, but something I've learned is that people who are excited about the idea of writing their first book have a lot of general questions about the book writing *process,* and they're more comfortable if they get answers sooner rather than later. So let's spend the next chapter on those FAQs—Frequently Asked Questions.

2

FAQS: FREQUENTLY ASKED QUESTIONS

You're asking: What is book writing going to demand of me? What will it be like? What am I getting myself into? The same practical and basic questions always come up. Let me try to answer them for you.

HOW LONG DOES IT HAVE TO BE?

As a child, I looked at fat books and wondered how the writers managed to find so much to say. To me, something like "The nutty captain tried to catch a white whale, and almost everyone died" would tell the full story, and I'd have nothing more to add. But Herman Melville made *Moby-Dick* out of it. How did he do that?

It's one of the first questions asked by someone thinking about writing a book: How does the writer find so much to say? How is the length of a book determined, and how long does *my* book have to be?

Writers and nonwriters have almost opposite attitudes regarding length. Writers know the problem is almost always too much length and not enough shortness. *Long* is an indiscriminate outpouring of raw material; *short* is a polished final product. Mark Twain famously apologized for writing a long letter, saying he hadn't had time to write a short one.

But nonwriters worry that they won't have enough to say. Their problem is largely that they haven't changed their way of thinking in a fundamental way: from *summary* thinking (the way *I* thought about *Moby Dick*) to *story* thinking (the way Melville thought).

Here's a summary (clearly *not* a story) of your life.

> *You were born. You went to school. You had a fist fight with a kid named Eric. You played varsity soccer and went on family vacations. The night of the senior prom, your car somehow collided with a telephone pole—no one was hurt, and you remember it with a smile.*
>
> *You went to the U, married, got a job, changed jobs four times. The kids were born. You moved to Portland. Dad died, then Mom. You became a grandparent. Now you're retired.*

That's it in two paragraphs. Flesh it out with a few facts, and your autobiography-as-summary is barely *two* pages long. That's a little too brief for a book.

A *story* is entirely different. What if I told you that each *sentence* of the two-paragraph autobiography above was now a chapter heading. Being born is a chapter. Memories of school days is a chapter. The fight with Eric is a chapter (and I bet it's a good one). And so on. Open any of these chapters in your memory, and the memory-movies start playing in your mind, and soon massive detail is coming back at you.

YOU DON'T HAVE TO BE FAMOUS

The problem is not too little, it's too much. Could you write a thousand pages? The answer is yes, for sure, but we all know that a thousand pages is not only unmarketable, it's unbearable.

There is no magic number of pages. Many factors—but primarily the structure you choose and the amount of memory and imagination you set free—will lead you to the final total. I think you're better off without thinking about length, but if you find you need to focus on a number—perhaps as an aid in developing the scale and level of detail of each chapter—then let's arbitrarily choose 120 double-spaced pages, mainly because 120 divides neatly into a dozen ten-page chapters (or ten twelve-page chapters).

A ten-page chapter should not be intimidating, and, believe me, you will *not* have trouble finding the material for a dozen such chapters.

Can you write a ten-page chapter about your parents or your kids or your career? Of course you can. And you'd just be getting started.

If you're thinking about writing only a twenty-page survey of your life, that's fine. Just scale down everything I say, as if your chapters were only two pages long. Or scale up if you want to go longer than 120 pages.

Don't fret about length. It's not an important issue as you get started.

But here's one relatively minor consideration. If possible, keep your chapters about the same length because if chapter length is always changing, you risk a rhythm or pacing problem. By that I mean that if you condition readers to eight-page chapters but then mix in a twenty-five-page chapter, they might find that the long chapter seems to go on forever. This does *not* mean that you should try to force a chapter worth twenty-five pages into eight pages just to be consistent—the content of the story takes priority over any considerations about the length. Look for a creative solution; maybe the long chapter can be broken down into three short ones, or maybe you'll decide later to lengthen the short chapters.

HOW LONG WILL IT TAKE TO WRITE THIS THING?

Make a reasonable estimate of how long you think it will take. Then triple it. Writing projects always take a lot longer than expected, because writing refuses to cooperate with your ideas of efficiency and time management. If you decide, "I'm going to finish chapter fourteen on Tuesday, starting at 10:00 A.M., in time to go lunch with Herb and Myra at 12:30," all I can tell you is that Herb and Myra will have to wait. They might have to wait a week or two.

Here's another way to look at it: Writers always say that one good page a day adds up to a book a year. If your idea of a book is 120 pages, one page a day equals *three* books a year.

WHERE AM I GOING TO GET MY IDEAS?

People always ask writers where they get their ideas. The answer is *everywhere*.

Research is an obvious source of ideas and I'll talk about research in a later chapter, but here's a hint about my thinking: Anything that's not *writing* subtracts from your limited and valuable writing time. Research is a gluttonous time consumer, and it's not terribly cost-effective in that you tend to use only a small percentage of what you find.

YOU DON'T HAVE TO BE FAMOUS

So my advice is to spend a minimum amount of time on traditional external sources—documents, albums, scrapbooks. The best ideas will come from your mind and memory. You'll get the most benefit from research if you think of it as a source of ideas, not facts.

Writing your autobiography will give you a new respect for memory, most notably the abundance and generosity of memory. While certain memories might be repressed, refusing to leave their dark hiding places in your mind, the vast majority of memories feel lonely and forgotten. They long to be rescued from oblivion, taken out and dusted off, examined carefully, and put to use.

There is very little problem with access: All you have to do is sit quietly in memory's waiting room, and in no time at all, the doors will swing open, and out they'll come. The quantity, depth, and detail of memories is just amazing, as is the sophistication—multimedia sounds, sights, smells, tastes, physical sensations, and the most subtle emotional reactions. You quickly realize that retrieving memories works by links and associations and connections. One thought or feeling or sensation leads to another; one scene leads to the next.

Think of memory as a spectacular search engine. Type in a topic and the search will retrieve a countless number of mental Web sites for you. Tapping into memory will give you not just a *lot* of material but virtually *unlimited* material. You can return to the same topic day after day, always finding new things. This is a bonanza, and all you have to do is allow it to happen. Of course, finding the meanings of memories and the words to describe them is something else entirely.

Conversations about autobiography and memory usually lead to lists of "sparkers"—subjects that call up memory files. Virtually anything and everything can function as a sparker, but let's make a quick and random list to prove it.

The alphabetical list I've made up below is random and not scientific in any way. If you made a similar list, it would be totally different. But if you focus on each word for just a few seconds, you'll understand its potential for releasing memories. Your concern about finding ideas and material will probably be replaced by concern about *managing* all the ideas and material accessible to you.

A: automobiles, asthma, arithmetic, airplanes, autumn
B: babies, blood, bosses, brother, beaches, baseball, birthdays, Bush
C: cats, cowboys, cancer, childbirth, Cadillac
D: Dad, dogs, deals, dancing, diets, death, Disney, diploma
E: elections, Eiffel Tower, Elvis
F: football, falling, fireplace, fishing, finance, fights
G: ghosts, grades, grief, guilt, girls in summer dresses
H: home, hot dogs, holidays, hospitals, hair, hobbies, heartbreak
I: illness, insurance, innocence, India, Israel, Italy, Iraq
J: jazz, jewelry, jail, JFK, Japan
K: kitchens, kisses, karaoke, Kris Kringle or Kristofferson
L: lost, lawyers, lawn, legs, lions
M: Mom, music, mountains, marriage, Mexico, macho, marijuana
N: nephew, necklace, neighbors, 9/11
O: Oscars, Ovaltine, ocean, Oldsmobile

p: pizza, Pontiacs, pools, police, poker, pets, prom, picnics, parties

q: quiz shows, Quebec, Queen Elizabeth

r: rodeo, rock and roll, Reagan, rain, raspberries

s: sunsets, summer, saving, sister, steak, snow, school, storm, speed

t: teachers, tank tops, toys, trains, trees, tragedy, Thanksgiving

u: uncles, United States, ultrasound

v: Virginia, violence, vice president, Visa, Vietnam

w: weight, wine, weddings, war, winning, West

x: ex-husband, ex-wife, X-rated

y: Yankees, Yosemite

z: zoo, zonked, zany

One other thing about ideas: The desired time for ideas to arrive is before you start writing or during the writing, but sometimes they come *after* a writing session. For example, it's thirty minutes or three hours later, and you're making dinner or playing with the cat or just daydreaming, *but your mind is still working on the book*. Suddenly, ideas are flowing, one after the other, the product of a relaxation and clarity you didn't have when you were working intensely at your desk. Don't dismiss these ideas because they come at an unexpected or inconvenient time; grab a pen and paper and make notes quickly before they float away.

What Does Writing Look Like?

People are always curious about the physical details of writing. If they are thinking about writing a book for the first time, they seem to require a mental image of how they would look in action. What will I wear when I write? Will I sip tea or smoke a pipe? What room will I work in? What tools will I use? Will I start with the dawn or labor in the wee hours of the night? Or just hang out in the kitchen?

I'm not sure why people (including me) want to picture the scene of a writer writing. Interviews with famous authors almost always include questions about the author's writing habits, as if the externals of writing would somehow give clues to the internals.

I've been in rooms where great writing has taken place, and there is a kind of tourist's delight in visualizing the author at work—Churchill stalking around as he dictated to aides, the three Bronte Sisters scribbling away together around their small dining room table, Wordsworth sitting on an uncomfortable wooden chair in the middle of an upstairs room as he gazed out a window at England's Lake District, Charles Darwin evolving his theory of evolution as his dog lay snoozing in a little wicker basket in the corner. It is difficult to avoid wondering about some magical chemistry between the author and the room, though, of course, the magic in the room took place invisibly in the writer's mind and had nothing to do with the wallpaper.

I offer myself as an example of how mundane the outward image of writing usually is. I sit at a table and poke away at a desktop computer. Sometimes I have a cup of coffee in my hand. I put the cup down when I need the hand for typing. When the cup is empty, I might or might not refill it. If you were watching me in action, that's what you'd see. It's no wonder I'm not selling any tickets.

But in those articles I read, writers always seemed to come up with eccentricities, perhaps to humor the interviewers. The writer would sharpen four #2 pencils and align them carefully at the upper right corner of his desktop. Or he would replace the

YOU DON'T HAVE TO BE FAMOUS

lightbulb in his desk lamp, screwing in his lucky writing bulb. Or he would play specially chosen music, perhaps hot and steamy Latin numbers, to get his blood pulsing and energy flowing.

Perhaps he would write standing up—Hemingway did that, but he also wrote seated at tables in Parisian cafés. Proust wrote in longhand while lying in bed. Some popular novelists write by dictating into a tape recorder, which allows them to sit, stand, walk around, or pedal exercise bicycles. Ancient Romans wrote on thirty-foot scrolls of papyrus.

I once read an interview in which Dick Cavett told of writing a book at his house on Long Island where he enjoyed the short commute to work—the walk from downstairs to his upstairs writing room. But as he was trying to develop momentum with the book, he realized he was fooling around too much, thumbing through magazines or balancing his checkbook, having a hard time getting around to writing.

Finally, it occurred to him that being comfortably at home in at-home clothes—jeans and a T-shirt—just didn't feel like a working situation. He needed to feel like he was in the office. So he got in the habit of dressing up to write—putting on slacks, a good shirt, necktie, and even a sports jacket to get into a professional mood. He said it was strange to get dressed up just to go to a different room in his own house, but it made the difference.

Most writers have their own prewriting habits, rituals, and idiosyncrasies, and they are inconsequential except that they begin a sequence that leads up to the ice-breaking moment when they write that first sentence of the day.

A common ritual among speechwriters, for example, is to put off the beginning of a new speech by searching for quotations. Most of these quotations are never used, but the writer just doesn't feel secure and ready to start without a page of quotes from Albert Einstein, General Patton, or Yogi Berra.

If you need writing rituals, work out your own. They're helpful. Otherwise just do whatever's comfortable.

SHOULD I SHARE MY ENTHUSIASM WITH FAMILY AND FRIENDS?

You might want to share your enthusiasm about your book, issuing daily reports and updates on your writing progress or getting into dinner table conversations about it.

Bad idea.

In the formative stage of a creative project, all your ideas are undefined, and you are extremely vulnerable to outside influence. Even the most casual nudge can push you drastically off course or onto a wrong course. A relative's remark, such as "So how are you doing with your *tell-all* book about our family?" might seriously chill your developing attitude about how you'll write about your family. Even something like "Wow, I can't wait to read all the funny stories" might give you the idea that your future readers are expecting rollicking comedy, which is not at all what you have in mind.

You shouldn't hear *anything* like this. You should do the equivalent of stuffing cotton in your ears to make yourself deaf to all such comments. I suggest that you work out a personal public relations strategy with the goal of deflecting any messages that could affect your writing.

The essence of this strategy would be keeping the lowest possible profile for your book activity. Don't bring it up in conversation, but when it comes up anyway, give polite but bland answers. If you need to ask research questions about the past, get your answers without volunteering much about how you're going to use them.

Be secretive but pretend that you're *not* being secretive, because secrecy creates mystery and invites peeking over your shoulder. If people probe for details, say you haven't reached that part of the story yet. If people ask to read what you're writing, put up a brick wall of defensive self-deprecation: "Oh no, I'd just die if anyone read the mess I've got at this point, but I'd love to have you read it later."

By "later" you mean when the book is done.

It's impossible to know how family and friends will react to you suddenly becoming an autobiographer, but it's a sure thing that everyone will be interested in what you are going to write *about them*. This could get very political, very tricky. *How much* will you say about them? Will you say *more* about Howard than you say about Henry? Will you tell stories that embarrass Emily or flatter Florence? Who will come out looking good and who won't?

Think about how petty, jealous, and downright ugly families sometimes get when fighting over the estates of deceased members. In a worst-case scenario, the struggle to influence your book could escalate to something along those same lines, even breaking out into open family combat in which you are lobbied, cajoled, quizzed, emotionally bribed, and threatened with dire consequences if certain people aren't mentioned adequately or reverently, if certain anecdotes are not included or excluded, if a particular historical interpretation or spin is ignored, if one sibling is treated affectionately while another gets barely a nice word.

You might start getting the idea that everyone has a different agenda in mind for your book and your idea about telling your story the way *you* want to tell it will not be greeted with enthusiasm. This is probably an exaggerated reaction, which you should resist. I think the book *will* be welcome, and highly welcome, but remember that it has to exist before people can read it and relax enough to enjoy it—while it's still a work-in-progress it might seem threatening because no one knows what you're up to. This creates a state of suspense in which people concoct wild and overwrought anxieties. In all likelihood, the final Richter scale rating on the book will be low compared to the earthquake that could happen before anyone reads a word.

I'm hoping your situation won't be anything like this. I just want to alert you to a worst possible scenario that you should exert yourself to avoid. Once the bad stuff starts, there's no stopping it, so you have to nip it in the bud or before the bud.

Radiate no-big-deal harmlessness. Keep sending a message that there's nothing to worry about. Be as boring as possible and hope everyone loses interest and leaves you alone.

As for concerns about how people will react when they actually read the book, that's a different matter, and we'll get to it later. For now, focus on sealing yourself off from even the mildest and most unintentional meddling.

WILL I EMBARRASS MYSELF WITH BAD PUNCTUATION?

I'm constantly surprised by how self-conscious people are about punctuation.

Perhaps they were all humiliated and traumatized by the same grade school teacher. That old witch did a lot of damage.

My advice: Do not let punctuation anxiety inhibit your writing. However, at some point you must pay serious attention to correcting punctuation errors, which will be embarrassing when people read your book.

Don't let yourself fall into the no-punctuation, no-upper-case style of e-mail or text mail. After a paragraph or two, this becomes intolerable to most readers, especially older ones.

Do a little brushing up. I suggest reading *The Elements of Style* (Fourth Edition) by William Strunk Jr. and E.B. White. It is 105 pages long, and you can read it in a day or so; you'll enjoy it. At the other end of the spectrum is the colossal *The Chicago Manual of Style*. The fifteenth edition is 956 pages long, and you can probably finish reading it the next time you circumnavigate the Earth in a rowboat. I suggest you keep it on your desk as a reference.

A few other quick points:

★ Use a lot of periods, and use them sooner. That is, write short sentences. Short sentences don't tolerate flab or sloppy thinking. They add punch. The Russian writer Isaac Babel said, "No iron can pierce the heart with such force as a period put at just the right place."

★ Some writers get Comma Fever and throw them in everywhere. Comma Austerity is better.

★ A well-used semicolon replaces a conjunction; it's a nice rhythm changer and adds muscle. Semicolons are most at home in formal writing; your autobiography is moderately informal, so use them sparingly.

- ★ If you are beyond junior high school, it's time to banish the exclamation point from your punctuation repertoire. There is no surer way to mark yourself as amateurish. Never use them. The only thing worse than an exclamation point is three exclamation points. Someone said using exclamation points is like laughing loudly at your own jokes.

- ★ Work on creating the impact of exclamation without the points. Put the strongest words or ideas at the end of sentences to create the exclaiming effect: "I worked hard, and I won" is more exclamatory than "I won after working hard."

THE BIG QUESTION (WHY?)

I've given you answers to some easy questions about book writing. Now let's move on to a different kind of question, and the answer must come from you.

In the next chapter, I'll discuss your motivation for writing your autobiography—what *you* get out of it. A related question is what do *readers* get out of it? That is, what is your *purpose* in terms of your impact on readers? What are you trying to tell them or get across to them? *Why* are you addressing them?

I think I can best describe this point about purpose in the context in which it first became clear to me, speechwriting. In seventeen years of writing speeches for CEOs, I repeatedly learned to ask what I call The Big Question—"Why are we giving this speech?"—in early meetings with the speaker-to-be and his or her assistants. This question seems almost simpleminded,

YOU DON'T HAVE TO BE FAMOUS

and it always takes people by surprise because everyone has assumed there is an obvious reason for the speech. Far from it.

Sometimes it takes only a short conversation to expose many different concepts about the speech's purpose. Often these purposes conflict. Sometimes you realize there is no purpose at all, except that the speaker said yes when invited to fill a place on a meeting agenda.

The writer listening to these conversations has a sinking feeling because he knows that writing *requires* a single, clear purpose. Secondary goals can be accommodated, but one goal must be primary. Don't trap yourself with a choice among three bad alternatives: multiplicity of purpose, ambiguity of purpose, or absence of purpose. You cannot start off in *multiple* directions any more than you can go to the grocery store and the post office at the same time. It is even more challenging to go in multiple directions *ambiguously* (being *intentionally* ambiguous, however, is a clear strategic direction). As for *absence of purpose,* this is a nonstarter, a writer's block situation of the first magnitude, comparable to getting into a car and driving with your eyes shut.

I have learned, in corporate situations where a speech's purpose is undefined, that I will have little chance of writing successfully until this problem is solved. So I reluctantly go into Bulldog Mode, stubbornly re-asking The Big Question but rephrasing it so I don't sound like a compulsive maniac ("What's the point we want to get across?" "What do we want the audience talking about as they walk out?" "What do we want them to remember when they go to the office Monday morning?").

When the answer finally comes, I pounce on it, repeating it out loud in as many ways as I can imagine. If possible, I would repeat it through a megaphone while forcing the speaker and anyone else involved to take a blood oath agreeing that this is the why of the speech because if there are doubts about the purpose, they will come back at me later and cause no end of trouble.

I do not mean to imply that finding your purpose is rocket science. It's not always difficult, but it's always necessary. And *finding* it is only Part A; Part B is to *keep your eye on it* when writing, as a helmsman might steer for a particular landmark on a distant shore. You need a compass and a course, a reference for all the decisions you'll have to make, from small word choices to major matters of content or meaning.

When the question is what to say next or what topic to cover next, consult the purpose. When you're not sure if something is relevant, consult the purpose. When you're not sure how to handle the ending, consult the purpose.

You do not have to be eternally committed to your purpose. Once you get momentum, you might see it in a whole new light. If that happens, don't hesitate to alter it, even if it means rewriting or reconceiving on a serious scale. But never be *without* a purpose or muddleheaded about purpose, and never just start jabbering away, hoping it will lead to something. What it's most likely to lead to is a waste of time followed by a feeling of being hopelessly lost.

The feeling of direction that guides you in the writing process can be implicit or explicit. By implicit I mean that you've haven't consciously thought out the answers to big questions about where you're going and why, but you do know the answers in an unarticulated way.

However, what I've learned is that when rough spots inevitably come along, and you really need an immediate

YOU DON'T HAVE TO BE FAMOUS

source of guidance to get back on track, implicit answers might be elusive. In the midst of a writing crisis, you don't want to be groping desperately for answers to fundamental questions about direction and goals. Therefore, even if it slows you down briefly before you plunge into writing, it's wise to put some early thought into developing explicit answers, always with an option to modify them later.

Knowing your purpose and having a sense of *what* you're trying to accomplish will steer your efforts on a paragraph-by-paragraph or chapter-by-chapter basis, but the essential, overarching element of directional clarity is knowing *why* you're writing. What is your *motivation*? The solution might be simple, but you should know exactly what it is. We'll focus on this in the next chapter.

MOTIVATION: FOUR GOOD CHOICES

You should know *why* you want to tell your life story. Don't be vague about it. Don't do it just because it seems like a good project, an interesting hobby, something to chat about with your friends.

Even if you plan to write only twenty pages, autobiography is a commitment, and you should not go into it unfocused. You should be able to state your reason for writing it *out loud* in a single sentence. Maybe write it on an index card and pin it to your bulletin board. And believe it.

Knowing your motivation is important because autobiography can be a complicated journey, and you need to keep yourself intellectually and emotionally on course. There will be moments when you say, "I've completely lost my sense of where I'm going with this, and why I'm even doing this." In those moments, it will be a lifesaver to consult with that simple statement of purpose.

I'm going to suggest three excellent motivations for writing your autobiography: discovery, posterity, and history.

And then I'll add a fourth, which is more about the process itself than the final product: fulfilling your creative impulse.

They are all good motivations, and you don't have to exclude any of them. You can choose one or all or any combination or add other purposes of your own. But just as a ship can have only one captain, a single goal must be first among equals.

You must be able to say, "I'm doing this to discover things about my life," or "I'm doing this to pass on something to the future," or "I'm doing this to preserve things from the past," or "I'm doing this to give my mind a stimulating workout."

REASON #1: DISCOVERY

In the summer of 2004, Bill Clinton went on a book tour to sell his newly published autobiography, *My Life*. I came upon this quotation in a newspaper account of a Clinton appearance:

> *I really think that anyone who's fortunate enough to live to be fifty years old should take some time, even if it's just a couple of weekends, to sit down and write the story of your life, even if it's only twenty pages, and even if it's only for your children and grandchildren. . . . You'll be surprised what you find.*

I agreed emphatically. In fact, it was this paragraph that gave me the idea for this book, though the thought of writing an autobiography was not new to me or others.

But don't overlook Bill Clinton's last sentence: *You'll be surprised what you find.* Nonwriters tend to think that writing is a struggle with words and writing rules in which you attempt to transfer *already-formed* thoughts from your mind to written language. This view does an injustice to both the challenge and rewards of writing and to the incentive to write, which is, mainly, *discovery*.

Writing good prose might be our immediate preoccupation as we work, but writing is more than a prose process, it's a *thinking process*. Writing drives you to create and develop ideas in a way that probably would not happen if you just sat in a chair and thought. At its best, writing is *not* about transferring already-formed thoughts to paper but about developing or generating ideas—building new thoughts in the process of articulating them.

Writing makes you smarter and more creative. I've always thought there was a loose comparison with arithmetic—we don't get very far doing calculation in our heads (most of us can barely add two double-digit numbers), but when we write it down on paper, our capacity expands by many dimensions. Words on paper help us advance and find directions that might never have been anticipated at the start of the page or paragraph.

Writing harnesses the power of concentration and engages a miraculous mental process that leads you to *discoveries*. Some of these discoveries are thoughts you've developed with rigorous and logical concentration. Others are random and seem to arrive suddenly like gifts from the deepest archives of your mind. Memory turns out to be a hard disk drive from which no file was ever erased. Writing helps you get access to these files. Memory cannot be coerced, but as I've said, if you relax and give it time, it will begin to do its astonishing trick of pulling level after level of fabulous prizes out of deep storage.

These memories are discoveries in themselves, but when you subject them to examination under the writing process, they have the potential to shape insights about your life. They might cause you to understand your life in a completely different way. They help you transform experience into knowledge and wisdom. They might fill a void in your understanding of who you are as you create a new level of *hindsight*.

Hindsight reveals things we didn't see when the past was the present. Things you haven't thought about in years—and never expected to think about again—will bubble up with amazing impact. Sometimes these revelations will be large and nebulous, but other times they might be quite specific. Let me give an example.

I recently came across a note I'd received years ago when I was a young, aspiring journalist. It came from an important executive, the chief of correspondents at *Time* magazine, who'd asked me to submit writing samples, on which he'd complimented me. In this note, he invited me to drop by his office sometime and "have a talk."

What memory tells me now, as if I'd just gone forty years back in time, is that I interpreted "have a talk" as nothing more than "have a talk." We'd had a few pleasant conversations, and it was nice that he was inviting me to have another one. What did not occur to me was that the "talk" he had in mind was probably a prelude to a job offer as a correspondent for *Time*.

The magazine was then in its glory, and a correspondent's job would have been a to-die-for career opportunity. But I was young and missed the signal. Re-reading this slightly yellowed note four decades later, I realized what a dramatically different course my life might have followed if I'd been a little bit more alert. Talk about a discovery.

Sometimes what we retrieve from memory are items that seem minor at first but then light up to illuminate important times, like cinematic flashbacks. Obviously, memories like this are packed with discoveries that are ideal for your autobiography.

Here's another example, a fragment of memory that always comes to mind when the December holiday season rolls around.

I have had Christmas trees almost every year of my life, and I've forgotten all but one of them. My mother believed in getting the biggest tree possible and overloading it with ornaments and decorations. She maintained that the concept of modest sufficiency did not apply to Christmas trees, which should express unbounded joy and abundance. Unfortunately, this placed a physical burden on the tree itself and required that the heavily laden tree be kept securely upright, which was no sure thing, given the flimsy tree stands of the 1950s when I was a teenager. I faintly recall that the tree at the center of this story had seemed a little wobbly, but in our holiday optimism, we were not alarmed and did nothing.

The moment of disaster arrived as I sat reading in a living room chair, and my dog, a beagle, walked near the tree. Without the dog, this scene would have been far less memorable, but as movie makers have discovered, it adds comic enrichment to place an innocent bystander in the middle of a stunning visual event—for example, a sign painter on a tall ladder who reacts in horror as a car chase wipes out his ladder, leaving him stranded in midair with his paintbrush poised for a stroke that will never happen.

The dog trotted past at just the moment the tree chose to abandon the vertical. Its fall began with mesmerizing and majestic slow motion. But the dog quickly sensed that the tree was coming down in her direction. Her escape reflex kicked in, and she took off in a terrified and undignified scramble.

My mind snapped a photo of the dog looking over her shoulder with panic in her eyes as the tree seemed to pursue her, but she was moving at survival-instinct speed and evaded the crash, still running as flying ornaments shattered on the floor and a cacophony of breakage seemed to go on forever. What a scene. I watched in a state of frozen amazement and then burst out in riotous laughter.

Today, more than a half-century later, I can call up this image with pinpoint clarity. It is like the curtain rising on a darkened Broadway stage, the lights coming up from dim to dazzlingly bright and sharp high definition, revealing a detail-perfect mental photo of a living room I last saw in my early twenties.

I can see the red rug, the two cream-colored couches, and the pair of black, iron floor lamps I still own. I can see the beloved dog, and, though they were not part of the scene, I can see my parents as they were at that age. And I can see myself and remember how it felt to be looking at the world through teenaged eyes.

Except for the mess, the fall of the tree had no consequence even then. We put it back up, this time wired so securely that a typhoon wouldn't knock it over. Of course, the dog would not go near it.

So is this scene significant in any way, or just a miscellaneous memory based on an old mental snapshot? I think it is significant. The proof is not only its durability but its rich evocative power, the detailed visual and emotional memories it brings back so freshly and fully. I should emphasize that memory made this choice; my conscious mind was not consulted. And of course, it was a far better choice than the standard scene I would have devised otherwise to describe the Christmases of those years.

The next question is, would the story of the falling Christmas tree be interesting to readers of my autobiography? My thinking is that if I worked hard to recall the scene and describe its meaning as well as its details, readers would see it and feel the same things I felt as I discovered a lost-in-time moment that still pulsed with vitality. Meanwhile, I could use that moment as a jumping-off point, holding the image in my mind as I described my home and household, my parents, my dog, and myself at that time of my life. Instead of being just an isolated fragment, it could be a way of backing into a scene that covered an entire period in my life.

Would I—then or up until now—have thought of this scene of the falling tree and madly dashing dog as something I would include in the story of my life? Not a chance. The memory had popped up in my mind many times, but I didn't really discover it until I wrote it.

"You'll be surprised what you find."

Warning: Blotting Out Your Memories

In my first college creative writing class, I wrote a story about my Ohio grandfather giving me a pony. It was a stretch from what really happened—I never got the pony, for one thing—but the story was a sensation. I had calls from the student literary magazine begging to publish it. My teacher helped me submit it to several real (nonstudent) magazines. It was my first and purest moment of writing glory and my high-water mark as a fiction writer.

But I paid a price I never expected: I lost the truth. I had been over the story so many times in my imagination, molding and changing it, re-arranging its facts, that by the end of the

YOU DON'T HAVE TO BE FAMOUS

process, the true memory had been revised so freely, I couldn't distinguish between what was real and what was made up.

Later I learned that this is common. When you write about a real event, you superimpose the new made-up version on the old memory, and the old memory is buried underneath, forever inaccessible. The grandfather I remember today is the fictional character I created, in the words and images I created. My memory of the real grandfather is gone.

So as you prepare to write stories recalling old memories, don't be surprised if this is the last time you will see those original memories intact. This should be an incentive to tell those stories with a maximum of accuracy and care, taking minimal literary liberties.

REASON #2: POSTERITY

*Let us now praise famous men . . . of others there is
no memory; they have perished as though they had
never existed; they have become as though they had
never been born.*

So it says in Ecclesiastes 44:1. But why should the great and famous get all the posterity and leave the rest of us with nothing?

Let me propose a rewrite.

*Let us now praise unfamous men and women; they
are remembered because they were written about,
even if they had to do it themselves.*

Look, we're talking about a very humble degree of posterity, perhaps extending our voice (in a written version) a decade or several decades beyond our lives, enough to be read by our grandchildren or great-grandchildren. But who knows? Anything can happen, and maybe our book will turn up in an attic a century from now and provide future generations with a valuable account of how their family lived many years earlier.

I think we should be remembered simply because we lived. That is our qualification and our message for posterity: *We were here*. What counts is surely not our achievements, which will be forgotten in short order, but the resonance and humanity of our voices, revealed and preserved in our writing. So we have to make sure that we select stories from our lives that have enduring human appeal.

You can read letters or diaries written two thousand years ago, and they are as fresh as yesterday and very much worth reading. I have some letters written by my parents before and just after they were married. The letters are vibrant with youthful optimism. I would quote from them in my autobiography. They capture a time and feeling in a way that would make their selection obvious and their posterity merited.

But if posterity is your goal, you have to be intelligent about what posterity values. A friend has told me with disappointment about a private autobiography written by his father, who was a highly respected achiever in several fields—a university president, head of a foundation, and chairman of a major government board. The book is so dry and matter-of-fact—sort of an *official* autobiography, a litany of accomplishments and milestones— that the man beneath the biographical details is never glimpsed. The reader finds out *what* he was, not *who* he

YOU DON'T HAVE TO BE FAMOUS

was. My friend shrugs with regret and says the book is simply not readable.

As I was working on this book, I visited an island in Maine and took a hike that included an old country cemetery. I found myself standing at the grave of a woman who died in 1886. The words "Gone but Not Forgotten" were cut into her tombstone. A nice sentiment, but, except for a weather-beaten tombstone, she is gone and forever forgotten. This seems sad. She was among the people in Ecclesiastes: *perished as though they had never existed.* She should have written an autobiography.

REASON #3: HISTORY

History and posterity have much in common as motivations for autobiography, but here's a distinction: Posterity is about *preserving*, and history is about *retrieving*. There is something heartbreaking about losing history—and therefore something hopeful about catching it on its way to being lost and yanking it back.

Long before I encountered Bill Clinton's quotation about autobiography, I'd thought about trying to preserve some sort of history of my life for my children, who, so far—both are in college as I write this—have shown little interest. This is disappointing, and I'm hoping it will change by the time I get around to writing my own autobiography. In the meantime, other parents have assured me it's common, and that their kids are the same way, somewhere between oblivious and fiercely *incurious* about their family's past.

Okay, I reply, but won't there come a time in later life, perhaps when they become parents themselves, when they get over this, a time when sister phones brother and asks, "Hey, didn't Dad spend a lot of time one year writing his autobiography? We all thought it was a goofy thing to do, but I'd like to read it now. Where'd we put it?"

Personally, I would be thrilled to encounter any such account of my own parents' lives. What were their childhoods like? What were their parents and their households like? Would I have liked them as young adults? What did they care about or not care about? What were their goals and dreams? Were they like me or very different? What were the shaping events of their lives?

But of course, it's too late. Sure, a few family anecdotes were fondly passed on, some photos and old letters remain, and a few living relatives have fading memories. But it could be so much better.

I hope I'm correct that there will be a day when the kids get interested. My worry is that by that point, I'll be gone, or perhaps I'll still be here, but my *memory* will be gone. Ninety-nine percent of the story will be lost.

Losing all that history is the way it's always been, but the upside is that preserving it by writing your autobiography—think of it as leaving a personal time capsule—is more doable than ever.

Think of it in terms of yourself: You are probably better educated than your ancestors and presumably more capable of writing. You will live longer than they did, meaning you'll have a longer retirement and more leisure time. You can design a far more comfortable writing experience, taking your laptop to the beach or sitting in your home office. Research questions that might have sapped the patience or ingenuity of auto-

YOU DON'T HAVE TO BE FAMOUS

biographers twenty years ago can now be answered in short order via e-mail or the Internet.

Pursuing your history will take you back in time, and perhaps *way* back. You will probably find yourself contemplating your roots; many autobiography enthusiasts are attracted to the genealogy angle. Genealogy can be fascinating, and perhaps even more fascinating is DNA genealogy, which promises to yield information about ancestors who lived hundreds or even thousands of years ago.

Without question, genealogical information would provide a structure for a family history, or at least a chapter. But autobiography or memoir writing goes *way* beyond the bare bones of a family tree. It might be interesting that you had a forebear named Ezra Jones who lived in Pennsylvania from 1823 to 1879, but that's probably as much as you'll ever learn about old Ezra.

Of course, I would back off this position if you told me you actually had substantial information about past generations of your family—some families have been pack rats throughout the generations, amassing mountains of old stuff. This could provide material for one or more good historical chapters at the start of your autobiography.

But few of us have such information. I suspect that our ancestors have been much like my kids, only casually interested in the vanished worlds inhabited by earlier generations of family. For some, it's more than low interest: Most Americans are descended from immigrants, and immigrants tend to have left their homelands because of poverty or persecution or other reasons they are in a hurry to forget.

Celebrating ethnic roots has become popular recently, but it's not that many years since the goal was to become

American as fast as possible, shedding all traces of the old country. It would take major investigation to follow the faint tracks of emigration, and the effort might not be rewarded. In the meantime, it would probably sidetrack the goal of autobiography.

So my advice is to go light on genealogy. Put the historical facts in order as well as you can. Rescue them from being forgotten and give them whatever attention they deserve.

But put most of your attention into narrowing the focus to *your* experience and *your* history, which will pay off handsomely. Remember the words of Shakespeare's Henry V in his famous prebattle "We few, we happy few, we band of brothers" exhortation:

> *Old men forget; yet all shall be forgot,*
> *But he'll remember with advantages*
> *What feats he did that day…*
> *This story shall the good man teach his son.*

REASON #4: FULFILLING YOUR CREATIVE IMPULSE

In chapter one, I discussed advantages that amateur writers might have over professionals. Let me add one more: In the professional process, everything is shaped by the goal of finishing, but the amateur doesn't have to think that way. The professional's motivation is reaching the destination, but the amateur can be motivated by the journey alone. Amateurs can do it purely to enjoy the feeling, satisfaction, and mental exercise of creativity.

People *need* to be creative, and Americans might need it more than ever, or may at least need to find time to pursue it. I have seen statistics indicating that the number of nonprofessional American writers is increasing every year. More than eight out of ten Americans say they want to write a book.

I think creativity should be regarded as a necessary daily workout for the mind, a calisthenic for the brain. For people over fifty, it should be integrated in a day's activity just as physical exercise is integrated. A little creativity, a little tennis or fishing, and your day becomes a lot fuller and better.

I had a wonderful and eccentric uncle named Perry, now deceased, who retired too early. One moment he had been a high-powered owner of a small business in New York City, caught up in bustling competition, deals, numbers, details, relationships with customers and employees; the next minute he was in Florida with nothing to do.

He was desperately restless. He was not a reader or a golfer or a boater. He had no hobbies. He didn't know what to do with himself. His family and friends were concerned because he was clearly not content. After considerable deliberation, they came up with a consensus solution: paddleball.

Perry had been a good athlete as a young man, and he liked sports. The thinking was that paddleball would be just right for him. It would be good exercise, and he'd widen his social circle by making friends with other paddleballers.

He gave it a try but couldn't stay interested. The family was disappointed, and I overheard criticism of him, behind his back. I remember defending him, "Hey, this man doesn't want to live out his life hitting a ball. He needs to have something to do with his mind."

But he couldn't find it. He was not an ordinary retiree, and no ordinary activity would do. He was not going to learn Italian or master French cooking. Instead, he would jump in the car and drive off in an anxious daily search.

He went to the courthouse to listen to trials. He spent hours at the airport, chatting up the counter people because he was fascinated with the idea that every ticket to Florida had a different price, and he wanted to be on the spot to follow price fluctuations. He got involved with a few local small businesses, always becoming valuable because of his advanced skills but reluctant to take on full-time commitment.

The family was slightly uneasy when he became an adviser to a motorcycle store—the retired senior citizen from Manhattan hanging out with a rough crowd of young, Southern bikers. Despite the culture gap, they apparently enjoyed his company, perhaps recognizing a kindred spirit, an out-of-sync loner who could not find his place.

All of these were short-term interests, and his problem was never solved. I was not thinking about autobiography in those years, and it never occurred to me to suggest that he should try writing. Most likely his restlessness would have doomed the effort. Further, in a family of good talkers, he was notably inarticulate, and often seemed to be frustrated by the weight of thoughts he could not express.

He repeatedly told me how much he wished he could be like me, a writer to whom words presumably came easily. And yet in the rare times when he got rolling, talking about the old days, he would light up with humor and tell his stories masterfully.

Now—too late of course—I'm thinking that autobiography might have been just the thing for him, a focus

YOU DON'T HAVE TO BE FAMOUS

for his energy and thoughtful intelligence and a way to wage a battle against inarticulateness.

But if I'd ever proposed book writing to him, I know just what he would have said: "Nah, I'm no writer. I could never do that."

True, he was not a writer. But could he have done it anyway? I think so, and I think it would have been rewarding. He would have loved the discovery and the history, and we all yearn for a bit of posterity. Above all, I bet, he would have enjoyed the mental exercise. An active mind needs worthwhile activity, and autobiography fills the bill in many ways: It will stir your imagination, awaken your memory, concentrate your thinking, rouse your creative spirit, and confront you with invigorating challenges as small as a good sentence and as large as something you thought you could never do: write a book.

YOU NEED AN ORGANIZING PRINCIPLE

If you're going to write a book about your life, it might help to decide what to call it. Choose from *autobiography, life story,* or *memoir*.

I admit to a bias against *memoir*. It is too French for me, too Old World, and too literary. If you asked me what *I* was writing, and the most accurate answer was a memoir, I don't think the word would come out of my mouth. Ingrained American resistance to pretentiousness would bring my teeth clamping down on my tongue somewhere between the *mem* and the *wahr*.

And yet *memoir* is used by many unpretentious and excellent writers, and the form clearly has its advantages. Memoirs tend to be anecdotal and episodic, going right to the most interesting parts of a life while sidestepping the duller parts. It is an approach worthy of serious consideration. If you want to write a memoir-style book but share my problem with the word *memoir*, use *recollections* instead.

I don't see a big difference between *autobiography* and *life story* and tend to use them interchangeably. I've used *life story* in the title of this book, hoping it will be less intimidating than *autobiography*.

My only reservation about *life story*—and maybe I'm being too literal in this complaint—is that while all of us have stories, few of us have consistent story lines to our lives, by which I mean a single theme that connects most of the things we want to write about. Such themes might include a personal or professional quest, a struggle with a disease or handicap, a powerful relationship, or a life guided by a sense of mission, faith, or higher purpose. Make a quick survey of your life, and if a single theme arches over it, you've found your story line structure.

As for *autobiography*, it does seem to suggest large scope, a formal and chronological structure, and hundreds of pages of detail covering everything you ever did. This is probably much more than you want to write. It's certainly more than most people want to read.

And since the usual expectation in a published autobiography is an upward curve that rises to a peak of fame and high achievement, it might be disconcerting for readers to find those elements absent, as they would be for most of us you-don't-have-to-be-famous writers.

Nevertheless, I keep coming back to *autobiography* because I think it implies a straightforward, personal history with no obligation to sustain a theme or live up to the literary expectation of a memoir. And forget about covering everything. Just cover what you want.

Contemplating the differences between *autobiography/ memoir/life story* is useful for only one reason: It makes the point that there are different ways to approach writing about your life. You can select any of the standard models or customize your own, but you should put some thought into it because the approach you choose will influence how you write and organize your book.

You need an organizing principle, a consistent angle of entry and attack, a structure that stimulates creative thinking, guides you in selecting content, and helps you impose order on your narrative.

This chapter suggests several approaches with the hope that you'll recognize one of them as right for you. Even if you don't, the discussion will make you more aware of how forcefully form shapes content.

Readers seldom notice or question the structural design of what they're reading, unless it's conspicuously faulty, but writers know that success is less about words and paragraphs than about a good, solid structure that reflects your purpose and motivation.

THE CHRONOLOGICAL MODEL

This is the baseline, the time-honored autobiographical model, and the model most people will instinctively choose. No structural innovation is required, and you never have to wonder about what comes next. You just follow the progression of your life, from birth to now.

To give us an example to focus on, I've written a few paragraphs showing how my own autobiography might begin. As I think back to it, what jumps out to me is that the opening chapter of my story would coincide with openings of new periods in family and world history. World War II had just begun, and my mother and father, married for only a year, had relocated to New York City after living in Ohio. The Ohio and New York sides of the family came together

YOU DON'T HAVE TO BE FAMOUS

for the first time, giving me a remarkably diverse background, especially by 1942 standards. I decided to begin my chronology before I was born, with my grandparents.

My maternal grandparents were Episcopalians from Ohio and Kentucky. Their roots reached back to very early America. My grandmother was related to the heroic Revolutionary War spy and patriot Nathan Hale. My grandfather also claimed a family connection to a Revolutionary icon, Betsy Ross, the seamstress who was said to have made the first American flag. The story about Betsy making the flag is now discredited, and my grandfather's story about being related to Betsy was dismissed by my mother, who believed it was a fib he made up to compete with my grandmother's Nathan Hale connection.

In contrast to these Episcopalians from Ohio, my paternal grandparents were New York City Jews whose families emigrated from Poland and Romania, where they lived what I imagine to be Fiddler on the Roof *existences. Indeed, the celebrated director and choreographer of the original 1964* Fiddler *production, Jerome Robbins, was my father's cousin.*

Jerome Robbins was painfully shy, and I never saw him at a family gathering. My one and only conversation with him took place when I spotted him sitting alone in a pizza restaurant in a Long Island resort town in 1983. He seemed pleasantly surprised to meet me, his cousin's grown-up son, and asked me to sit down. He was waiting for friends to join him; they were going to see the movie E.T., which had just opened.

I asked about his memories of a trip to Poland in 1924 when my grandmother and his mother took him and my father back to see the Old Country and meet relatives still living there—almost everyone they met would later die in the Holocaust. I had always had it in my mind that Robbins's impressions from that trip had been the inspiration for Fiddler. *But he just laughed and said, no, he couldn't remember a single thing about the trip; he was only six years old at the time. That had never occurred to me.*

My mother gave birth to me in a Jewish hospital in New York City, where an unscrupulous rabbi came to her bedside, and, speaking in a thick accent she couldn't understand, fooled the trusting girl from the Midwest into signing a contract to buy an expensive encyclopedia, which, he assured her, would rescue her baby from a life of ignorance. The family resolved the matter by recruiting an enforcer who was sent to make the rabbi a counteroffer he couldn't refuse, and the encyclopedia deal went away.

Only a few months before my birth, the newlyweds had moved from Ohio (where they met as students at Ohio University) to New York, where, three days before the attack on Pearl Harbor, my father was hired as a newswriter by CBS Radio, a job which would shape his career and our lives going forward.

So in a period not much longer than a year, my parents had relocated, my father started a broadcast news career that lasted until the end of his life, my mother gave birth to her only child, and America entered a world war—a war which, at the time of my birth in May of 1942, offered anything but certain victory.

So there's the first page or two of a meaty first chapter. It sets the stage for my birth by telling a little bit about family history, even including a cameo appearance by a celebrity, Jerome Robbins. It touches on two favorite family stories—my grandfather fibbing about being related to Betsy Ross and my mother being hoodwinked by a rabbi. It locates the story in time—the young couple setting up in New York as the world went to war overseas. It establishes a fundamental point about my identity as a product of very different cultures—Ohio and New York, American and immigrant, Protestant and Jewish—and it sets up numerous questions that would flesh out the rest of the chapter:

★ What is the background of the young couple's courtship and marriage? Why did my father go to college in Ohio? (He sent postcards to one hundred colleges to compare tuitions and expenses. The Depression had devastated his family's finances, and his goal was to find the cheapest college in America.) And how did my mother manage to become the first woman in her family to earn a college degree at a time when not that many women went to college?

★ How did the very different families get along? (Amazingly well.)

★ How did my mother adjust to the move to New York, which included a new ethnic family that regarded her as a lovable oddity from some distant cornfield in the unknown lands west of New Jersey? (She loved this role and played it with Diane Keaton verve.)

★ What was it like to be a young couple living in New York City during World War II? (I was too young to be paying attention, but my sense is that it was quite romantic.) What was it like to write nightly reports of the war's historic battles for a national audience when radio news was in its glory years? (Stories about how exciting it was were still being told years after the war ended.)

These are rich and lively subjects. They immediately begin the process of putting flesh on the bare bones of family history, turning facts into stories and signaling the reader that an enjoyable reading experience is ahead.

This chapter would create exactly what a first chapter should create: liftoff. *Launch*. Lots of topics and story lines could then follow, each of them leading effortlessly to even more topics and story lines. I could write many pages before getting around to my own birth. I might not even be born until the second or third chapter.

Something I've noted frequently in autobiographies of famous people is that the first half of the book—the author's youth—is usually far more involving than the second half, even though the second half is usually about the career or achievement that made the author worthy of a book. That is, the fame story is why you buy the book, but the *pre*-fame story is often more interesting. Why is that, and what is its relevance to our autobiographies?

I would suggest several reasons. One is that we already know about the writer's adult story, but his youthful story is new to us. Another is that youth is easy to relate to because we've all been there, while fame is

YOU DON'T HAVE TO BE FAMOUS

a subcategory of adult life, which most of us have never visited and which often turns out to be less fascinating than expected.

But the most relevant reason might be about journey versus destination. In childhood and youth, we are all travelers in a new and exciting world. Our destination is unknown and mysterious. Even small experiences along the way have powerful impact. Years later, we recall them vividly, and they seem to have greater resonance than the experiences of our adult years.

The journey is the Huckleberry Finn time of life when we encounter most of the defining events, memorable action, and imagery of a life—we have adventures, face dangers and obstacles and turning points, pursue passions and dreams, have victories and setbacks, make good friends and maybe enemies, play our cards right or wrong, win or lose or change course. (All of these, of course, are topics to be covered in your account of *your* journey.)

The destination, by comparison, is where we level off and experience the consequences of the journey. The pace of change slows down, and adult life presumably comes into long-term focus. Like it or not, we find out who we are. With luck, we're content with what we find. (Another good topic.)

It's different for everyone, but my rough guess is that the journey phase of life comes to an end in your middle-to-late thirties. There is still a lot ahead, but the drama of making our way is usually replaced by a more conventional script about careers, spouses, parenthood, and time speeding by—as the old saying about child rearing goes, "The days are long, but the years are short." Our future memories of this period might seem indistinct compared to the livelier details of the journey.

Does this mean that the early chapters of an autobiography will have a verve and richness that later chapters cannot equal? They might. You might discover that the book you want to write does not extend beyond a certain cutoff date in your life, or that the stories you want to tell come out of a single, highly memorable period—college, military, years when you lived overseas, marriage, the childhoods of your children. In *Life on the Mississippi,* Mark Twain looked back autobiographically on a period of four years when he was a young man learning to pilot steamboats; Antoine de Saint-Exupéry wrote an exciting memoir of his adventures in the early days of aviation in *Wind, Sand and Stars.* Neither felt compelled to cover his whole life; one short, memorable period was enough.

If your youth is what you want to write about, or if you find your writing enthusiasm dwindling as you move into your adult years, stop where you want. A few years from now, if you decide to tell the rest of your story, you can come back and write a second volume.

But if your decision is to stay with the start-through-now chronology, you should be aware that a journey-and-arrival transition in your life is likely to require a transition in the narrative style of your book. The events of the journey phase of your life stand out clearly and are easily recalled but when you look back at what I've described as the destination years, it may seem that long periods of time are a blur. They raced by *without* obvious milestones—we worked hard, raised kids, and overall it seems like nothing very notable happened. In our first efforts to recall these years, it might seem impossible to cull out any specific story

YOU DON'T HAVE TO BE FAMOUS

material other than a few obvious events such as gradua-
tions, weddings, job changes, deaths, and so on.

In your alumni class book you write, "Moved to Se-
attle. Raised two kids, Jimmy and Barbara. Worked as a
manager at Boeing for many years. Now retired." That
seems to cover it—forty years of your life in twenty words.
What else are you going to say about those years? How are
you going to write about them?

The answer is that your style has to change in a way
that parallels the change in your life. It becomes less about
hopping from one large formative event to the next and
more about reflecting, finding deeper layers of meaning
in smaller events, being more creative about the memories
you select and the thoughts that come with them.

The need to change your approach halfway through
your life story might take you by surprise. For people
whose lives have changed dramatically, the adjustment
can be major. What comes to mind are the lives of professional athletes. Reading their obituaries, I am always
struck by the thought that athletes seem to die twice—the
first death coming with the end of their playing career. To
obituary writers (or their editors), this first death brings
down the curtain on the athlete's newsworthy life, and the
obituary might end there, without a word about the years
between the athlete's last hurrah and last breath.

I always wonder: Did the old athlete have no life after his
years on the playing field? Did he dangle in limbo for those
last three or four decades? Perhaps he raised his children
and sold insurance until his mid-sixties and then retired to
raise tomatoes. Is that *nothing*? Did life lack all meaning after
he'd hung up the cleats? Obviously not—not to him, anyway.
The point is that his life changed, and if he were writing his

autobiography using the start-to-now chronological model, he would have to make a sharp transition from recounting the breathless glory days of his past to describing the slower-flowing and entirely different life that came later.

The idea about the eventfulness of your youthful years subsiding into a different kind of story as you get older is obviously a generalization—some lives get *more* eventful with time—but what I'm getting at involves a divergence between the autobiographical model followed by famous people and a model that will be suitable for unfamous writers.

I would suggest that Mr. Famous has an easier assignment. He does not have to probe around in hazy memory because the scenes of his fame are well outlined already. Readers know them and expect to read about them. His autobiography will be fundamentally journalistic, taking us through the highlight film of his life, lining up his great moments and describing them, perhaps fleshing them out with personal revelations and behind-the-scenes commentary or anecdotes.

The rest of us will not have that album of clippings to work with or that established record of events. This seems like a disadvantage. But on second thought, perhaps it's a strength.

Ten or twenty years from now—which might be the time when our books are most read and appreciated—the celebrity author's moments in the spotlight might be long forgotten while our description of years spent raising tomatoes and watching the river roll by will have timeless value and quality.

This means that if we're going to tackle the standard-model chronological autobiography, covering our lives from the start until now, we are going to have to part ways with the famous-autobiographer model as we blaze a trail of our own.

Of course, it will include the noteworthy milestones, but we will also discover as we search those stretches of time from which specific memories seem to have disappeared that *they have not disappeared at all*. They just require a little more archaeology in your memory before the rewards begin to emerge.

If you doubt this, spend some time in your basement or attic or open that old trunk that's been closed for twenty years. Wipe off the dust and touch that old tricycle or the wild Hawaiian shirt or the carton of business correspondence you brought home in 1993—you might have three great chapters suggested by those three items.

And, importantly, we'll come to understand that the absence of big events does not mean that nothing happened. The fabric of life is made up of countless small stitches, and each stitch is a possible story.

Here's an example of what I mean by a small stitch: I recall a summer evening shortly after my graduation from high school when, during a trip to Chicago, I walked by a department store and saw my reflection in its window and stopped in my tracks because I saw in my own image that I was no longer a high school kid but a young man, away from home and entering the adult world. Other window-shoppers stood next to me, looking at the merchandise, but I was looking at a life-changing perception: One part of my life was over, and a new time had begun.

"And Then I Did This ... and Then I Did That ... and Then I Went Here ... and Then I Went There..."

Based on the amateur autobiographies I've read, I think the most common mistake—the mistake most likely to damage the readability of your book—is becoming a slave to chronology.

You dutifully grind out your report on what happened this year and what happened the next year and so on, filling in the boxes of life's calendar but losing the bigger picture and perhaps the feeling and flavor of the life itself.

The success of your book depends to a large degree on your ability to see your story as something *more* than a procession of events, *more* than a daily diary as long as your life. If you start drifting in this direction, you should pick up a warning from its monotonous, laundry-list rhythm of event upon event: "And then in 1990, I did this... and then in 1991, I did that... and then in 1992, I went here... and then in 1993, I went there..."

What you *did*, for the most part, is only a framework for your life story. Don't mistake the framework for the substance. Events of long ago are probably not very interesting, to readers or even yourself, unless they *evoke* the times you're recalling, bringing them back to life and capturing their emotion and meaning.

Okay, how does a writer *evoke*? This question merits a few semesters of literature and creative writing classes, but instead, let's boil it down to the following two paragraphs, with more to come later.

Pretend you're walking on a beach with a son or daughter or friend, earnestly recalling old times. Concentrate on making your listener see and feel what it was like. *Show* the physical action or appearance of these scenes and *tell* what you learned from them or why you were affected emotionally. These meanings don't have to be deep or complex, and they certainly don't have to be poetically described—just put your finger on why they're worth remembering and describing. Create an energetic narrative and keep it on a level you can manage.

If you're writing about moving out of the old house in Des Moines, tell what you remember about the day. Tell how you felt when the moving van pulled up outside, how you felt saying good-bye to old friends and driving by your old high school on the way out of town. Tell why you moved and how your kids or parents felt about it. Describe your hopes and fears as you headed toward something new. Just do that, and if you do it simply and honestly, your evocation will be more than adequate.

VARIATION ON CHRONOLOGY: THE FLASHBACK MODEL

There is no mystery about how the chronological book would be assembled. Its viewpoint is strictly past tense and front to back. You start at the beginning and march forward, covering the milestone events but also letting memory roam, retrieving images and impressions and anecdotes that define those years.

But there is a variation on straight chronology. It's a bit more demanding but, in my view, much better because it gives you more flexibility and perspective.

Instead of starting in the past and inching forward, situate yourself *in the present looking backwards*. This means that the first pages of your book would deal with *today*, perhaps describing the circumstances of your decision to write an autobiography, surveying the place you've come to in life, talking about the present and even the future. It might be many pages before you turn back to the past. Your chapters might begin by taking advantage of something you didn't have years ago—hindsight. Tell why certain events or stories are worth remembering—what they mean *now* and what they meant *then*.

For example, it might be a good detail that in a certain period of time, your family always got together for Saturday-night poker games. But it would be even better if a discussion of your family *as it is today* led you back to an appreciation of those long-ago poker sessions and how they strengthened family bonds, linked the generations, provided fun and entertainment in a time when no one could afford to go out on Saturday nights, and illustrated the various personalities and characteristic conduct— Grandma's gentle patience, Larry's joke telling, Jennifer's explosive competitiveness, Uncle Tim's fits of sneezing, and Aunt Martha's tendency to sneak into the kitchen for nips on the vodka.

In some cases, you might find neat connections or patterns between then and now, but this isn't necessary. I've used the word *flashback* in the title of this section because the term is instantly understood by moviegoers as a memory sequence triggered by something that happens in the present. But I would caution that life is not as tightly plotted as movies, and connections that lead you with scriptwriter perfection to topics or memories from yesteryear are few and far between.

You shouldn't have to face omitting a good story from the past because you can't find a way to link it to something in the present. Nor should you create contrived or artificial connections between the old and the new, because such connections are false and inevitably break down.

But you will find that many good connections come to mind naturally if you spend a moment thinking about them, as the poker example illustrates. With each chapter, you would have the option of using a present-to-past structure or changing to past-to-present. This flexibility would keep you from falling into a rut of repeating the same structure in every chapter.

My preference would be letting the present lead to the past, but however you do it, the present *should* have a strong place in the book. How you see things *now* and the judgments you make on things *now* are essential to rounding out the story of your life.

THE EPISODIC MODEL

Some people will choose the chronological model simply because it seems like the right way to structure an autobiography. But the model you choose should fit your material.

Select the memoir or episodic model if you think of your book as a dozen or so chapters about subjects or memories chosen because telling these stories is what motivates to write your autobiography. They can be related or unrelated, chronological or not.

A friend told me about an uncle who wrote a thirty-five-page memoir covering four anecdotes from his life. My friend said they were wonderful stories, but there was no rhyme or reason connecting them. When he asked why his uncle had chosen these particular stories and why he chose only four, his uncle just shrugged and said, "Because that's what I wanted to do."

However, you might want to consider something slightly more organized. Readers prefer connectedness to miscellaneousness because they'd rather read a book that adds up to something greater than its parts. Having an organizing principle guides you in selecting the right stories to tell and helps you develop a consistent voice and storytelling structure, so you don't have to start from scratch with each chapter.

Here are some structures for autobiographies using the episodic model: *Recollections of Mom and Dad, My Times in the Navy,* or *The Story of My Marriage.*

Or how about: *The Twelve Best Days of My Life* or *The Twelve Most Important People in My Life.* These are both good episodic structures, and you should consider them.

Think about whether "best days" or "most important people" is the best way to categorize the story you want to tell. Make a list of most important people and best days to see if either idea seems promising (or goes flat).

A similar idea is *Twelve Turning Points in My Life*. Turning points are essential in any life story. Using turning points as an explicit organizing principle could be an excellent idea, but its flaw might be that while some turning points were obvious at the time, many of life's turning points sneak by without notice. You might have decided in a single illuminating moment that you wanted to be a pediatrician, or the ambition might have grown quietly over many years and with no specific cause. Turning points that happened without drama or imagery might be difficult to describe with the desired impact. They might even be difficult to remember—you might have no idea what made you want to be a pediatrician.

But the twelve-of-something idea (to fit twelve chapters) is promising and worth some thought. It could be twelve greatest decisions, twelve greatest accomplishments, twelve best friends, twelve lessons learned, twelve principles you believe in, twelve best teachers, twelve funniest real-life stories, twelve best trips, or twelve favorite pets.

These ideas might seem a long way from standard autobiography, but once you start writing, you might find that the structure might still follow a chronological sequence but the *selection* of material would be based on an organizing principle other than each year's calendar.

THE THEME-LINKED MODEL

At the start of this chapter, talking about the term *life story*, I said that some lives *do* have a single dominating theme or

YOU DON'T HAVE TO BE FAMOUS

story line, and if your life is in that category, look no further: Write about yourself and medicine, yourself and law, yourself and religion, yourself and your company, yourself and the Green Bay Packers, yourself and your garden, yourself and your household.

I have several friends whose lives have been devoted to journalism. They had long and engrossing careers as journalists, all their friends and travel and social or cultural interests are linked to journalism, and their view of the world comes through journalistic eyes. So a no-brainer solution for them would be *My Life in Journalism*.

I also think of a professor I knew as an undergraduate who always said there were three great loves in his life, "My wife, my church, and Stanford University." For him, I'd suggest another no-brainer: a three-part autobiography with long sections titled "My Wife," "My Church," and "Stanford University."

Other themes come to mind: triumphs and tragedies, victories and defeats, friends and enemies. I know a woman who, in her late fifties, look backs at a life whose theme, she thinks, is a series of amazingly bad decisions. Describing your life in terms of your worst blunders might seem like an odd idea but she is a good writer (with an excellent sense of humor), and she's working on an autobiography titled *What Was I Thinking?*

Are there big themes in *your* life?

THE HISTORY-LINKED MODEL

So far, we've been focused on the narrow world of ourselves, but there is a wider world out there, the world of great events and issues. In my lifetime, there have been eleven American presidents and several wars—World

War II, Korea, Vietnam, two invasions of Iraq, and numerous lesser military actions. I watched TV coverage of the assassination of President Kennedy, the landing on the moon, and the events of September 11, 2001. Many great plays, movies, and books have come out in my lifetime. There have been many thrilling moments in sports. I've read about horrible crimes, tragedies, riots, natural disasters, terrible diseases, and cures for diseases. Lots of history and history of all kinds.

What is our relationship to our times? How have these great events touched our lives? Even if their impact was not direct, you might be able to write a dozen chapters reflecting on them, recalling your reactions at the time, telling what you thought and felt and describing any action you took, any changes in your life that followed immediately or later, and how you regard those events as you look back at them today.

I had a memorable relative named Sonia Cullenin, a lifelong social activist and firebrand. At her ninetieth birthday party, with one hundred guests gathered in a lawn tent on a serene August day in Vermont, she gave a podium-pounding speech that barely acknowledged her birthday or the presence of her family and friends who had come from all over the world. Instead, she delivered an oration on the need to crusade for important issues, and she discussed some of her long history in doing so. It would not have been hard to work out a structure for her autobiography: *Twelve Things I've Fought For*.

THE STREAM-OF-CONSCIOUSNESS MODEL

Last, and probably least, comes the no-model model. You have no plan, no theme, and no structure. You spend no time working out answers to preparatory questions I've suggested. Instead, you just sit down and wing it, pouring out whatever comes into your head.

It may be part chronological, part episodic, part theme- or history-linked, essays about the cosmos, diatribes about your ungrateful children, or none of the above, or just a totally chaotic stream of consciousness.

You write a lot of pages, and at some point, you stop and read what you've written. Then you decide whether to keep going, commence serious editing, or switch to some other activity.

My bet is that you won't like what you've written. Undisciplined, unstructured, unedited prose might yield some spontaneous gems here and there, but for the most part, it tends to be disorderly and hard to put up with. Ignoring the basic rules and conventions of writing is an invitation to anarchy, and making anarchy readable is a challenge that exceeds the skills of most writers.

But perhaps that doesn't matter. Needing to write and needing to be readable are not always the same need. If stream-of-conscious autobiography works for you, go for it. There's always the chance that you will discover something that you would never have found with a standard approach.

PREPARATION ISSUES: RESEARCH, OUTLINING, SELF-DISCIPLINE

I'm assuming that your autobiography is *not* a full-time project. This means your time for it is limited, so efficiency is important. Any time you spend on this project that's not *writing* is subtracting from valuable time. Therefore:

★ You should limit the effort you put into research.

★ You should question the conventional wisdom of trying to outline your book before you start.

★ You should prepare yourself for serious self-discipline. I know that self-discipline is not always an inviting concept, but you can't write a book without it. Despite all the jokes about the misery of the writing experience, it usually becomes a pleasant and even compelling addiction. As Plato said, "The prisoner grows to love his chains."

RESEARCH—KEEP IT LIMITED

Research is essential in most writing projects, but let's keep in mind that you are not a historian or journalist with a responsibility for comprehensiveness and maximum accuracy. You have no obligation to be comprehensive, and while the credibility of your work always depends on its accuracy, you can be approximate as long as you're open about it. (That is, if you can't remember whether an incident took place in 1978 or 1979, you do not need to mount a major investigation. If a quick scan of family papers or an Internet search fails to solve the problem, there's nothing wrong with writing, "It happened in 1978 or 1979, but I'm not sure which.")

Research tends to become a pursuit in itself, and it can be a bottomless pit of time and effort. It will yield some nuggets, but most of it will be marginal. Unfortunately, you'll be tempted to use some or all of this marginal information *just because* you put so much effort into collecting it.

Research is also a great excuse for stalling. You never get around to writing because there is always one more call to make, one more Internet search to run, or one more fact to hunt down. You can be very creative about research, going through public records and scouting for new family sources, but there is always a price in time.

Possibly the biggest drawback is that if you do a lot of research and accumulate a lot of data, you have to put it somewhere. This means you have to create an infrastructure—a system to file and organize everything.

The history of systems is that they start simple and turn into monsters. They demand attention and management. And if they're not well designed, you'll actually make information *less* accessible. You won't remember whether Robert's fiftieth birthday party is filed under Robert, birthdays, parties, turning fifty, or 1998.

My view is that, for a private autobiography, at least 90 percent of what you need is between your ears. Let your *brain* do the research. Use research not so much for chasing facts but for jogging your memory. The old letters or photos or trophies or the sled with "Rosebud" written on it—these items trigger recall and help you form a vision of the past. So go up to the attic or down to the basement and look through your old papers and old cartons of junk. Do this once. Don't make a habit of it.

As for interviewing friends and family members to get different perspectives or interpretations of past events, there's nothing wrong with that, and it might add depth. It might also add conflicting opinions about what happened and what it meant. And you might find that inviting family members *in* to your autobiographical effort is easier than inviting them *out* and risks the complications I mentioned in chapter two.

Be low-key about your interviewing. Weigh its benefits against its costs in time. Don't let it distract you from your priority, which is to spend your time where it's most needed, sitting there *remembering* and *writing*.

INFRASTRUCTURE—KEEP IT SIMPLE

You do need an infrastructure, but keep it minimal. Like research, infrastructure management can be a bottomless pit. Some people can't function *without* infrastructures while others can only wing it. Do what's what best for you, but be warned.

I have fallen into the infrastructure trap more than a few times, setting up over-complicated filing systems.

YOU DON'T HAVE TO BE FAMOUS

Inevitably, by the end of the project, the system is a shambles, and I'm ignoring it, functioning in relative disorder and doing surprisingly well, thank you, but regretting the time I invested in the system in the first place. So the care and feeding of anything more than a rudimentary filing system is to be avoided.

Let me describe the simple system that's evolved for me. I'll put it in computer terms, but it transfers easily to pencil and paper. My first step is to create a file called *Notes*. Dump *everything* into it: big points and small, facts and fragments, chapter ideas, good words and phrases, images and anecdotes you want to think about later, thoughts about people to talk to or things to read, random names and numbers. Do not require a practical reason for saving a note—if something about it catches your imagination, keep it.

One morning not long ago, I woke up remembering the home telephone number of the apartment where my family lived until we moved just after I finished fifth grade. It amazed me that this useless fact had been in hibernation for so long and that it chose to emerge on a seemingly arbitrary morning *fifty-two years later*.

Because I didn't want to wait a half-century for another chance at this long-lost biographical tidbit, I hurriedly wrote it down and put it in my *Notes* file. Then I dialed the number, hoping for a *Twilight Zone* experience in which my mother, father, or I (as a twelve-year-old) would answer. No such luck. The number was IL 9-5592, but if you're calling after 1954, forget about finding me at home. The number now belongs to a home care agency.

When I recorded the number in my notes, I had no idea how I would ever use it. *But I'm using it right now* to illustrate the unexpected value of keeping accessible notes of old memories.

One memory leads to another. The memory of that phone number led me to a memory of an old black telephone and the stubby little wooden table it sat on. I remember that phone ringing in 1949 when my grandfather died, and my mother sat down in the dark foyer of our apartment and cried, something I had never seen. I remember it ringing on the night of March 4, 1953, when Stalin died—my father was a CBS radio news editor, and his newsroom thought he should know right away. My mother and I stood around in our pajamas at 3:00 A.M., watching him take the call. My father muttered a few choice words about Stalin and went back to bed.

While your *Notes* file will obviously be chaotic and packed with things you won't use, it has the virtue of locating all notes *in one place*. As time goes by, you'll do some pruning and impose a modicum of order. You might find yourself moving items around to group related items in the same place. Sometimes you'll insert emphatic marginal notes or put key words in colors or boldface.

When you sit down to work on a new chapter, go through the whole file and pluck out every item that might possibly be useful. Copy it into a new file called *Notes for Chapter Five*.

You might also want a file for writing you've deleted. You tell yourself you may want to use it elsewhere, but the reality is that you worked hard on it and just don't want to throw it away. I call this file *Outs* (as in outtakes). I almost never resurrect anything from this file, but I keep it just in case.

YOU DON'T HAVE TO BE FAMOUS

Of course, you also create a file called *Chapter Five*. If you want to keep your sanity, this file and *Notes for Chapter Five* will be the *only* files you pay attention to when you write.

When you're working, never stop to search for any fact or quote or reference unless you're sure you can locate it in a matter of seconds. The risk is that you'll find the fact but lose your chain of thought. E.B. White, the wonderful writer who, with his former professor William Strunk, became the coauthor of *The Elements of Style*, said that writing often "becomes a question of learning to make occasional wing shots, bringing down the bird of thought as it flashes by." Instead of losing your bird or chain of thought—which might be unrecoverable—just make a note and pursue the fact later.

Finally, you do not want to lose anything you write to a technological glitch, so become a maniac about backing up files. My computer automatically backs up the file I'm working on every three minutes. Every time I leave my desk, I close the file and copy it to a floppy disk. Almost every day, I back up everything to a hard disk. On Saturday mornings, I copy it all onto a CD. If I could think of ten more ways to back it up (other than printing it out), I would. All this backing up has almost never done me any good, but I'm convinced that the day I stop, the hard disk will die, and everything will be gone. So I'll never stop.

One more thing: All writers know that once you're focused on a writing project, almost everything you encounter in the course of a day seems to be relevant, warranting inclusion in the book or sparking ideas or revisions. Sometimes these out-of-nowhere ideas are true offers from your subconscious—the trick is writing them down before the offer is withdrawn. I've learned that despite the strongest vows to remember these things, I'll forget them unless I make a note within a few seconds. My solution is to be permanently armed with a 3 x 5 index card. Sometimes, the mind starts sizzling with ideas, and I scribble them down in the smallest handwriting I can manage. Later, I transfer these notes to the big *Notes* file and throw the cards away. The last thing I want to do is contend with hundreds of semi-legible index cards.

TO OUTLINE OR NOT TO OUTLINE?

I've never been much of an outliner.

In my corporate speechwriting career, I've been asked several times to submit an outline for discussion and approval before I begin the first draft. My answer is a more diplomatic version of, "I write speeches, not outlines." This idea comes as a stunner to executives, most of whom are process-minded managers who believe in outlining as an article of faith. They cannot comprehend working *without* an outline.

As they gaze at me in wonder, trying to absorb this alarming divergence from all that seems rational, I add, "I tell you what, I'll give you an outline *after* I write the speech, but not *before*." This offer, with its cavalier cart-before-the-horse logic, seems even nuttier than no outline at all, but I explain that an outline made *after* the writing would demonstrate that the speech passes the test of outline logic even though no outline was followed when it was written. (No one has ever remembered to ask for the postspeech outline.)

I think the big question about an outline is: *What do you want from it?* Do you want to generate ideas or just line up existing ideas in an orderly sequence? If you want to organize ideas you've already had, an outline is fine. But outlines are not good at *generating* ideas. They are *not* good at stimulating fresh viewpoints or approaches. In fact, I think they *constrict* creativity.

As you prepare to begin a writing project, generating ideas is a far greater priority than working out their sequence. Therefore, trying to create a detailed outline *before* you have the ideas is ill-advised.

A good outline will be useful in numerous situations *later*. At a certain point, the organization of your book will start coming into focus, and you'll make structural outlines as you go along, refining them frequently. Outlining also helps when you want to say three things at the same time and need a solution or get bogged down and lose focus or want to preview the coherency and logic of a sequence.

But I'm against *early* outlining because this is the prime discovery phase when your imagination should be unconstrained, random, and wide-ranging. Give memory and creative momentum a chance to spark unexpected ideas and directions.

This might seem to conflict with what I've said about being prepared and knowing your purpose before you start writing. Not really. Knowing your purpose is different from having specific ideas about execution, and the worst thing you can do is to cut off future discovery by limiting yourself to the plan prescribed by your outline. And when I advise against having an early written outline, I'm presuming that some notion of your structure—an *unwritten* outline—is evolving in your mind. But it will be very simple, something like: "I'll start with A, that'll lead me toward B, and maybe the ending will be C."

This stage in the writing process, where nothing is too defined or confined, is often where the best writing begins. It's where *creativity* shows up. The creativity of writing a book is something different from the creativity of building a bridge. Building a bridge is an engineering challenge, and an outline is a perfect expression of an engineering mentality—determine the necessary elements and devise the right sequence of steps to implement them. Book writers will have to deal with structure and sequence soon enough, but first come the unpredictable and often illogical inspired notions, spontaneous digressions, tangents, free associations, and flights of fancy.

The author Joseph Heller said his book ideas always started with random sentences that came to him out of nowhere. He was lying in bed when he thought of, "It was love at first sight. The first time he saw the chaplain, Blank fell madly in love with him." *Catch-22* sprouted from that sentence. Another out-of-the-blue sentence ("I get the willies when I see closed doors") led him into his next novel, *Something Happened*.

On the few occasions when I've had to work with a full outline, I've noted that somewhere around Roman II, Para B, Subpara I, I realize that what I'm doing is not really writing at all. I'm *executing the outline*, painting by the Roman numerals. When you're only providing prose to flesh out the outline, you realize that you've abdicated creative control. The creativity that's going into this project has *already* been spent: It went into the outline. Then it stopped, *before* the writing started.

This is bad news because outlining is so inferior to writing as a creative process. I would wager that very few imaginative ideas have originated in the outlining process.

Those out-of-nowhere lines that energized Joseph Heller would never have survived—the outline mentality would not have known what to do with them and would probably have discarded them without a second thought.

I'm now going to call a surprise witness to support my argument: Sigmund Freud.

On a trip to London, I visited the house where Freud lived the year before his death in 1939. A replica of the Vienna office in which he founded psychoanalysis has been constructed in a downstairs room of the London house— the actual couch, the real chair where he sat listening to patients, his collections of books and antiques.

In a display case is a card printed with Freud's answer to a question about how he worked at his crowded desk. His answer, not quite to the point, was, "When I sit down to write and take my pen in my hand, I am always curious what will then follow, and that drives me imperatively to work." The exhibit card, reflecting an interpretive psychiatric mind-set, then adds, "The forces at work in producing the narrative remain unclear until the end."

I laughed out loud reading that card. Here was one of the greatest scientific thinkers of history, one of the foremost experts on the workings of the human mind, admitting that he picked up his pen with no idea what he would write but was eager to learn his own thoughts, which would "remain unclear" until he finished composing them.

Freud knew the only way to discover exactly what he wanted to say was by allowing the writing process to open his mind and refine his thoughts. An outline wouldn't help because he didn't know his destination in advance and therefore could not outline his route. The only way to get to what he wanted to say was by taking up his pen and engaging the writing process.

So now you're giving me a hard look and thinking: Okay, that's dandy, *but how am I going to write my book without an outline?* Without an outline, how will I know where I'm going and what to write next?

My favorite quotation on this subject comes from the novelist E.L. Doctorow: "Writing a book is like driving a car at night. You only see as far as your headlights go, but you can make the whole trip that way."

Face the fact that you can't outline the whole story because you can't see that far. Your headlights don't reach that far. Focus on what you *can* see and let it lead you forward. Your combined concentration and creativity will start revealing ideas, directions, and structural solutions, and it'll be richer than anything you would have outlined. This is how you find a path in the darkness. But, of course, the darkness isn't *that* dark. You know how your stories come out because you've lived them. The basic outline is already in your head.

Until you get well into the book, use only an unconfining, rudimentary chapter outline, perhaps so rudimentary you don't need to write it down and use it as a crutch. Or maybe use Roman numerals but ban the lower hierarchies of upper and lower case numbers and letters. If you're using the chronological model, try something as simple as this:

    i. Birth
    ii. Childhood
    iii. High School
    iv. College
    v. Twenties
    vi. Career
    vii. Family

    YOU DON'T HAVE TO BE FAMOUS

VIII. Midlife

IX. Now

Once you get rolling, each chapter will assume a rough structure, which you can then refine.

A final thought. If you disagree with me and feel you can't work without a detailed outline, you'll have a lot of company, and that's fine. If you go the outline route, I recommend an old writing trick in which you prevent the outline from dictating to you by getting it physically out of your sight. Decide what to write—for instance, the story of the day the dog jumped out the window—and then turn over the outline page or close the outline file. Disconnect from the outline. Break your mental dependency on it. Force your mind to digest the thought and process it freshly and originally, rather than just repotting it. Don't let the outline do the writing.

Personal Chronology Up Front

This idea is not original with me, but I think it's a good thing to do: At the very start of the book, between the title page and page one, insert a single page giving a thumbnail outline of your life. You can do it by years, by decades, by milestones, by topics, or whatever. Just list the key dates and events. This will help readers form an overall picture of your life before they start reading, and it will be a handy reference they can flip back to.

More important, having this brief outline up front will relieve you of some of the burden of constantly clarifying chronology points throughout your narrative. It might help you relax somewhat from the duty to cover every event—the "Then I did this … then I did that" syndrome.

YOU NEED A WHIP-CRACKING TYRANT (YOU)

Remember Woody Allen's famous line, "Eighty-five percent of success in life is just showing up." Book writing requires showing up. It is imperative to get yourself into the writing position and to do so on a disciplined, regular basis. The longer the interval between writing sessions—when days stretch to weeks—the greater the likelihood that you will never come back to it.

Working on your own means you have to be your own boss, and not just a boss but a merciless, whip-cracking tyrant who accepts no excuses. "Go to your room," you'll tell yourself in a sharp, parental tone, "and don't come out for three hours."

It is a bizarre thing about writing that while writers are masters of evading it, they are also obsessed with not getting enough time for it. In what seems like a hostile conspiracy by the outside world, time keeps disappearing, and interruptions keep getting in the way. A phone call. A door bell. A kid's request. A security alarm three streets away or the clanking of the radiator in a way that could foretell an explosion if you don't run down to the basement right away. All these things seem part of a deliberate pattern to curtail your sincere attempt to put in working hours.

The novelist Catherine Drinker Bowen has said, "What the writer needs is an empty day ahead." Very true. It's a glorious feeling to sit down, knowing you've got a vast expanse of free time and can work unimpeded.

But the next move is to start frittering the time away. "A writer takes earnest measures to secure his solitude," says the novelist Don DeLillo, "and then finds endless ways to squander it."

Flaubert said, "Be regular and orderly like a bourgeois, so that you may be violent and original in your work." I'm not sure what he means by "violent"—perhaps he means passionate or unrestrained imagination—but I like this advice because he sees writing as a built-in element in a domestic routine rather than a spur-of-the-moment activity that happens only when you are seized by the muse.

The notion of writing only "when the spirit moves you" will quickly reveal how infrequently the spirit does any moving. *You* do the moving.

Heed Flaubert: "Be regular and orderly." Reserve time for this. At the appointed hour, you should report to your desk and remain there for a predetermined period. I read somewhere that if you promise yourself you'll be at your desk writing at seven the next morning, your brain starts preparing for that session, and it will be on time—but your body has to show up, too.

As I've gotten older, I've discovered that stamina is an issue. Intense concentration for hours is increasingly difficult with age. I used to be able to sit and work as long as I felt like it, including deep into the night. In my sixties, that open-ended capability has disappeared.

My goal now is to do about two hours at a time. After lunch, my energy dips and I'm useless for several hours. I try to do three two-hour sessions a day, maybe a fourth at night. I understand that you might be able to fit in only one such session a day, but you can make a lot of progress in two hours if you don't waste time.

There are many days when you put in heroic effort but have little to show for it, and other times when you work feverishly on something that seems like a masterpiece of world literature until you read it the next day and recognize drivel that has to be fed to the shredder as fast as possible. This is part of the game.

Determine your freshest, quietest, and most interruption-free time of the day and be tough about resisting interruptions. Most writers are larks who flourish in the early morning, but many are night owls. Figure out your best writing time and keep to it, inflexibly.

Discourage friends and family from approaching you in that period. Unplug the phone. Don't look at the mail, and by all means, don't open e-mail. Put the magazines, catalogs, and other distractions in another room. If necessary, relocate to a place where you can't be easily reached or distracted, such as the town library.

(I've seen a University of California study showing that businesspeople are interrupted every eleven minutes, and after an interruption it takes them twenty-five minutes to return to the interrupted task. I doubt if people working at home are interrupted that often, but there's a strong warning in the twenty-five-minute figure: One or two of those, and your writing session is as good as gone. And who knows what productive chains of thought are lost forever.)

Determine how much time you need to get into the flow and do some good work before running out of time. I would say you need a *minimum* of two to three hours if you're trying to generate new material. If you're revising, you can get a lot done in a shorter period.

Don't make it too arduous, or it will wear you out or overtax your discipline. That plan to write all day Saturday is attractive, but it probably won't happen. Don't get in the habit of making promises you don't keep—it only gets worse.

6

WHO ARE YOU AND WHO IS THE AUDIENCE?

It's no small point that autobiographies are written in the first person. Someone named "I" is the central figure and does most of the talking. Who is this person? We know it's you, but does this *you* come through to the audience? And while we're at it, who is the audience?

Writing in the first person comes naturally to some, but most people find it surprisingly difficult. The freedom to be themselves and write in their own voice is a liberation they're not ready for. Except for e-mails and some letter writing, they have little experience with it.

They write a few pages and are shocked to discover that their normal, lifelong speaking voice does not transfer automatically to print. They re-read their first few pages and look up in dismay. *This isn't me.*

Instead of writing in their own voice, they seem to be writing in the voice of *some other* person. It's as if a stranger (who sounds like a high school sophomore) has inhabited their being. The voice is unrecognizable: uncertain, affected, erratic, and uncomfortable.

I've had speechwriting clients tell me they tried to write their own speeches but gave up in a fury because of this problem. "Why is this so damn hard?" they ask. "I'm a smart guy, but I cannot do this. I cannot get through half a page. What's the trick to this?"

The problem is that to write in your truest and most comfortable voice, you have to know who you are as a writer. You have to accept that when "I" starts talking, a character is being created on the page. You have to know how this character talks, thinks, and reacts. If you don't know, every sentence becomes a guess, an experiment. The resulting prose seems unnatural, unauthentic and somewhat unhinged, producing this odd feeling that someone other than you is doing the talking.

A writer needs to develop a writing self. We all have many selves—our parent self, our spouse self, our employee self, our one-of-the-boys or one-of-the-girls self, our old-friend self, and our new-acquaintance self, maybe a slightly different self for every role and relationship and situation. With each self comes a voice.

Voice is a writing term and a good one once you understand it. Some people initially interpret voice to mean only the *sound* of how people speak—the language they choose, vocabulary, mannerisms, tone, inflection, and so on. But how you sound is only part of it, the lesser part. The essence of voice is *who you are*—the character of the writer as encountered by the reader.

I have a speechwriting anecdote that helps bring this point to life. The first question people ask speechwriters is usually, "How do you capture a speaker's voice?" They

YOU DON'T HAVE TO BE FAMOUS

seem to think speechwriters have a secret process for imitating or adapting the way a client speaks and getting it down on paper, so the client can then stand up at a microphone and sound like himself.

Once in a while this is true. A few clients do have a distinctive way of talking, and if the writer's ear is good enough to pick up some of the client's characteristic cadences and word choices, that's enough to simulate the speaker's voice.

But (take it from me after seventeen years as a professional speechwriter) most people do *not* have a distinctive way of speaking. Just the opposite: They are *indistinctive*. You could listen to them for hours and never be able to simulate their voice on paper, other than repeating a few pet phrases. The speakers *themselves* can't write their own voice. This is what makes them so frustrated.

So when people want to know how I capture a client's sound, the answer is that in most cases, I don't even try. In fact, the sound that clients get from me is much closer to *my* sound than theirs.

What I try to capture is not speaking style but identity— how what they say reflects their personality, their position in life, their viewpoints and attitudes.

So here's an anecdote. I wrote a speech for the CEO of one of the Baby Bell telephone companies. Bell corporate culture is more than a century old, and one of its unwritten rules is that a boss should never act intellectually superior or do anything to suggest that he or she is better educated than other Bell people.

The Bell audience has an acutely sharp ear for violations of this rule. Even a tiny step over the line transfers the offender's name to a list of executives from whom full acceptance in the Bell family will be forever withheld.

I was insufficiently aware of this fiercely anti-smartypants strain in Bell culture and committed the maximum error by including in my first draft a quote from Shakespeare. I've forgotten which quote it was, but it was garden-variety, junior high school material. If I'd been *trying* to show off, I'd have chosen something much fancier.

But the quote jumped out at the CEO as if I'd slandered his mother. Not only did he strike it out with a big angry *X*, he was upset with me for putting it into a first draft. I should note that he was a well-educated man, not at all hostile to Shakespeare but not willing to sabotage his reputation with a flagrant breach of company etiquette.

I was seriously in the doghouse and needed a fast recovery. I remembered being told that the three most important things to the CEO were his family, the Bell system, and the Detroit Tigers. So my solution was to rip out the Shakespeare quote and replace it with a baseball anecdote.

He loved the baseball story and told it to the audience with comfort and good humor. It got a big, warm laugh, and people talked later about how funny Bill had been. The executive who'd hired me gave me a pat on the back and said, "Gee, you really captured Bill's voice. How do you speechwriters do that?"

A speechwriting mentor once told me that the challenge was to devise a *persona* for the speaker—*persona* meaning a clear identity that could be presented to an audience. The speaker would then *play himself* as if he were playing a role. Staying "in character" with this role would be his guide to how to speak and act, defining his "voice." A famous TV talk show host once told me, off camera, that he wanted to

YOU DON'T HAVE TO BE FAMOUS

quit smoking because "I would not smoke"—after a moment's confusion I realized that "I" referred to his public persona, who would not smoke because it would be out of character with his wholesome, healthy image.

Writing in the first person requires creating a character or persona for yourself, your normal speaking voice adapted to print. It has to be very close to your truest self because stepping into a fabricated identity would ring false. What you want is just a simplified, enhanced, consistent, and more distinctive version of yourself. You don't fake or consciously design this voice—the verb that's always associated with voice is *find*. You find your voice. It's in you already; you just have to develop it.

For most people, the finding process takes time and a lot of writing. Voice evolves. But you don't have time for this, so we'll speed evolution along by focusing on answers to two big questions that are factors in voice.

One is about getting a sense of the people you're writing for (*Who is your audience?*) because you will instinctively tailor your voice to your readers if you know who they are. The other is about content—most importantly, it is about deciding how openly you're going to communicate (*What are my levels of candor and disclosure?*).

WHO IS YOUR AUDIENCE?

If you're talking to your old college friend Mike, you know exactly what voice you'll use for the conversation. This voice was worked out long ago, and you can switch into it effortlessly. The same is true of the voice you use talking with your mother, your brother-in-law, maybe your clergyman, your long-time boss, and the three friends you've played golf with every weekend for the last twenty years. Separate relationships, a separate voice for each relationship.

But now, in your book, you will have to talk to them all *at the same time*, in a single voice. Will you talk to Mom like you talk to Mike, telling her the same things in the same way? Will you talk to your boss the same way you'd talk to your golfing buddies? Will your minister be amused by the same funny story that would crack up your brother-in-law, or would he be offended?

In print, you can no longer hop around among all your many voices. You have to commit to a single voice that fits the whole audience. Performers often say it's impossible to fathom the whole audience, so, instead, they concentrate on just one person they know well—the whole audience becomes boiled down to Uncle Ned, sitting in the first row with a big approving smile on his face.

On the other hand, in my days as a writer for ABC network news, I routinely wrote for television audiences in the millions, and at least one *20/20* audience was estimated at forty-five million. The diversity of an audience of that size dwarfs the imagination. I tried to keep in mind that I was trying to communicate with the elderly and the young, with neurosurgeons, cowboys, prisoners, dock workers, restaurant owners, accountants, gym coaches, students, Hispanics, Russians, hospital patients—an endlessly diverse list.

Given this enormous variety, the idea that Uncle Ned or anyone else was a typical viewer seemed ridiculously inadequate. The whole idea of *tailoring* seemed inadequate. All I could do was try to write as simply and cleanly as possible.

I've always thought that an excellent guide for doing this is Principle 16 of *The Elements of Style*: "Use definite, specific, concrete language." This principle is unglamorous and uncatchy, but it's the essence of serviceable craft: If you stick with "definite, specific, and concrete language," it's difficult to go seriously wrong.

What made writing for the vast TV audience a little easier was that I was writing in an established and impersonal journalistic style, rather than my own first-person voice. The autobiographer cannot hide behind an impersonal voice. However, as the author of a *private* autobiography, you do have one significant advantage: Because you control the book's distribution, you can define the book's audience. You won't just be tailoring your prose to the audience; you'll be tailoring the audience itself. For the most part, it will be an audience that already knows who you are and how you speak, so you're already part of the way to a good voice.

Total control over who reads the book is impossible once it is out of your hands, but the control you have is probably good enough, and you can exercise it simply by regulating the number of copies you make and who receives them. Ten copies ensures a small and tightly selected audience, one hundred copies could mean anything. Think of it as the difference between talking to a small group of friends in your living room or standing at a microphone and addressing an auditorium full of listeners.

While every audience member is different, your readers will have a lot in common, starting with the fact that they are all linked to you and your world. You may have to make some compromises at the edges—which probably means toning down or eliminating the racy stories or off-color language you would use with Mike while expanding the normally narrow range of topics you might discuss with Mom—but this need not cramp your style severely.

Because you'll know fairly precisely who your audience is, you'll be able to answer questions that will speed up the development of your writing voice. Are you talking to your immediate family—spouse and children—or the entire family, including all the cousins, nieces and nephews, uncles and aunts? Are lifelong friends part of the audience? How about newer friends from your career or community? How about the grown-up children of your friends and family?

Every widening of the circle indicates a less intimate voice. If you plan to post the book on the Internet, where anyone in the universe might read it, the voice requirement is going to be very different than the voice you'd use to address a dozen good friends.

How do you feel about having your book passed around and possibly read by people you don't know? How about your survivors, including generations not yet born? Maybe your voice has to be a little more formal or proper to be right for readers you will never know.

NO AUDIENCE BUT YOURSELF

You might choose to write your autobiography for *no* audience other than yourself. It might seem strange or surprising to take the notion of a private autobiography to this extreme—no readers at all, just you—but it certainly removes all ambiguity about your intent: The book is for your gratification and no one else's.

This releases you from several concerns that complicate the writing challenge. You are freed from all the usual

YOU DON'T HAVE TO BE FAMOUS

limits on style and content—privacy, taste, sensitivity, language, or anything else. You don't have to worry about finding a voice that works with multiple readers. You can range wide or go deep, you can tell all, you can make no effort to please readers.

But be careful before you go too far with this. Even if you print only one copy, you can never be confident that no one else will ever see it. Secrecy creates great temptation among others to find out what you've written, raising the possibility of espionage under your own roof. And in any of a number of nightmare scenarios—you're in a coma or confined to a hospital or dead—there'll be no one to protect its privacy.

For purposes of this and further discussion, I'm going to presume that your book *is* written to be read by other people. If it's to be read by an audience of *one*, such as a spouse or a grown-up child, that points you in a clear direction. You know this person, you have an established relationship and style of talking to this person, and you know what this person knows about you. The voice problem gets a lot easier.

Create an Imaginary Focus Group

In *King Lear*, Gloucester tells how he sees the world despite his blindness: "I see it feelingly." So be like Gloucester and exercise your imagination. Whoever your readers are, see them feelingly, as if you were talking to them face-to-face and could read their reactions in their facial expressions.

Picture your core readers—parents, spouse, kids, friends—sitting in a room reading your book. You hear a giggle from one corner, a grumble from another. You see riveted concentration on some faces, but you also notice a few yawns.

Think about the answers they'd give if a focus group "facilitator" walked in and started questioning them about your book. Try to determine what's holding their attention or boring them or putting them off. What is surprising them, entertaining them, hurting or offending or impressing them, making them chuckle or cry? What are they likely to *misunderstand* unless you make a diligent effort to be clear?

People intuitively adapt to whomever they're speaking to. We're all pretty good at it. The challenge for the writer is to find a way to do this when you can't *see* the people you're speaking to. Visualizing is the next best thing. A hazard for writers is getting lost in their imagination and wandering off on strange detours, but visualizing the audience will bring you back to some reality about the individual and collective identity of your readers. This will keep you from drifting out of character and out of your normal voice.

Creating an imaginary focus group will also guide content decisions. You might realize that certain anecdotes are screamingly inadvisable and should be dropped while others should be expanded or deepened. Remember that voice reflects not only style but substance.

The one audience member you cannot forget to please is yourself. You are the author but also the prime consumer—no one will give your book more attention or get more out of it than you. No one will have a better sense than you of when your voice is true or false, and false notes will bother you forever.

Voice is your intuitive solution to addressing your audience. Once you have it, it'll be like suddenly learning a new language. You'll re-read what you write and say, "That's me." The feeling that a slightly deranged imposter has hijacked your voice will go away as your own natural voice begins to emerge.

WHAT ARE YOUR LEVELS OF CANDOR AND DISCLOSURE?

Are you going to be self-censoring or free-wheeling? Where will you draw the line on sensitive material? How much will you protect the privacy and feelings of the people in your life? Will you keep secrets or reveal everything?

Unless you simply decide to steer around all sensitive topics—and this is an option many people take—your degree of frankness and openness can be a major issue in autobiography. I'll say more about this in a later chapter, but it's important to discuss it now in relation to voice.

If you are inhibited regarding candor and disclosure, your voice will reflect an element of restraint and keeping your distance from readers as you evade, avoid, euphemize, or pull punches—all of which can be done acceptably well as long as you don't call attention to it with blatant contortions (if skipping details or disclosures seems especially obvious, just admit it: "This is something I don't want to get into").

On the other hand, if you hurl restraint to the winds and move to higher levels of candor and disclosure, your voice will be much freer, more active, interesting, and colorful. An unrestrained book is much more fun to write and read than an uptight book. Of course the price of this liberated voice is the risk of a catastrophic reception when your book reaches its readers.

Let me pose some questions that may help you decide how to match your voice to your purposes.

★ Is your goal to create a dignified narrative of your life story that could be read by anyone without embarrassment? Or do you feel that there is no point to writing a book unless you're going to tell the whole story, warts and all, no holds barred?

★ Are you concerned about what readers think of you or would you rather tell it like it is and damn the torpedoes? Is your attitude that this is for posterity, so you'd better play it straight, or that you might be long gone when people read the book, so who gives a hoot how they react?

★ What boundaries of emotion, taste, and confidentiality will you observe?

★ To what degree will you express aggressive opinions or judgments?

★ To what degree will you discuss potentially explosive subjects like the Big Three—sex, politics, and religion?

★ What about language—the King's English, slang, four-letter words?

★ Are you willing to shock or outrage your readers, or do you very much not want to upset anyone?

★ Do you want to change your readers' opinions of you or reinforce them?

★ To what degree will your writing be affected by a disproportionate focus on reaction from a particular reader? (This is the inherent risk in the Uncle Ned Approach—a book aimed

YOU DON'T HAVE TO BE FAMOUS

at Ned as your typical reader will not be fair to Fred, Ted, and Ed.) Nor, I suspect, do you want your book to be dominated by your desire to impress your straight-laced former boss or to get belly laughs from your kids or to avoid offending a hot-tempered cousin who expresses disapproval with his fists.)

The answers to all these questions have to be right for you and fit your goals for the book. You should consider the answers in the abstract before you start writing. Specific cases might cause you to make exceptions later, but as you begin, it is advisable to have a thought-out *policy* on candor and disclosure.

A policy is a guide to consistency, and consistency has two great virtues. One is that it's an across-the-board solution that saves you from dealing separately with the same or similar decisions later on. That is, if you decide you won't *ever* discuss old romances or money problems, you'll have an easy decision each time either of those subjects is about to come up.

Second, consistency gives readers a sense of security while inconsistency is a red flag that marks you as erratic. Being consistent about a *wrong* decision at least shows that you did it intentionally and with the courage of your convictions; inconsistency, however, indicates that you are out of control or don't know what you're doing. That's when your readers put your book aside and never pick it up again.

Less is more is almost always good advice, and it's especially good when dealing with potentially explosive matters related to candor and disclosure. What seems to you to be a tiny, tiny, tiny bit of candor or disclosure can land like a nuclear bomb on the hearts and souls of your readers. Writers are often flabbergasted at how much unanticipated damage they've done, unintentionally. The key is to be aware of this possibility while developing a voice that is neither so inhibited it drains the juice out of your story or so frank and honest that readers are horrified.

HOW TO FIND YOUR WRITING VOICE

"Just be yourself" would be fine advice for mastering voice, but you don't know *how* to be yourself in print. In the same category of glib and misleading advice is "Write as you speak." This sounds good, but it doesn't work. If it did, people would not have so much trouble with voice. They don't know *how* to write as they speak, and, frankly, that's not the goal. The goal is to figure out how to *write as you write*.

One of the reasons people have so much trouble finding their voice is that they've spent years *suppressing* their voice by writing in an impersonal office voice—bureaucratic, academic, or corporate. Nothing could be worse preparation for autobiography.

Another problem is that when people encounter the absence of their own voice they often resort to imitation. Imitation is unauthentic by definition, and it doesn't work because the writer they choose to imitate is usually the most distinctive stylist they can think of, usually a superstar professional. Sustaining an imitation of a great performer is next to impossible, and this tactic fizzles out in a few paragraphs. So then, following a good instinct, they try to imitate *themselves* ("write as you talk"), ending up with an exaggerated version of their own worst qualities—their accents, habits, or mannerisms enlarged to the point of self-parody.

The next thought is: If my natural speaking voice is failing to transfer to print as a writing voice, perhaps it would

YOU DON'T HAVE TO BE FAMOUS

be a clever tactic to dictate my autobiography into a tape recorder and then transcribe it. My authentic out-loud speaking voice would thus be captured on paper.

This might work for some people, but for most of us, it won't succeed because talk and print are so different. If you've ever read transcripts of people talking, you've seen something that usually resembles a caricature of normal discourse. It is appallingly sloppy, disjointed, and fragmentary, full of unexplained references, leaps of logic, and truncated thoughts. It has no discipline and darts around, free associates, veers off on tangents (and never returns), uses horrendous vocabulary and grammar, and is so inarticulate you wonder how anyone could have understood it. This is painful reading, not what you want for your autobiography.

If I had to single out a category of writers who are masters of voice, I would pick newspaper columnists. They make you feel like they are sitting next to you, having a lively conversation with you. You know their personality and style and worldview so well that you can almost hear their voice coming off the page. Try to write like a newspaper columnist, and you'll develop a new appreciation for their skill. Actually what they do is a trick, a simulation of talk—if they sat next to you and read their columns out loud, they wouldn't sound nearly as right.

Some people would say that what columnists do illustrates "write as you speak," but it's really much more sophisticated than that. Instead of writing down what they might have said aloud, they're doing something much more sophisticated: They have learned to *write talk* or to write what the characters they've created for themselves might say.

This is what you have to do, but here's the big problem: The place where a developed voice is most needed is the place where voice is most undeveloped—the start of your book, when you introduce yourself to readers. You might evolve a decent voice by page 20, but you don't have it on page 1. Hence the severe discomfort that begins the moment you leave the starting line.

There is no magic remedy for this. The only thing to do is to muddle forward. You'll probably be aware of how awkwardly you're writing, but understanding the problem—your writing voice hasn't taken form yet—will make this a lot more survivable.

Once you're over the Himalayas of starting, you'll notice a gradual easing, a sense of naturalness slowly setting in. Sentences, then paragraphs, will start sounding like they actually came out of a human. You'll recognize the *you* that begins to emerge, and now and then you'll find yourself asking absurd-seeming questions like, "What would my reaction to this be?" or "Would the real me say that?" This, of course, means, "How would the writing self I've created react to this?" and "Does that language work for my writing voice?" Would I quote Shakespeare or tell a baseball story? Would an image like the "Himalayas of starting" ever come into my mind, and if it did, would I use it?

Your voice will get a little surer and more controllable with each hour of work. At some point, you'll look back at your early pages and realize you're now a lot closer to being able to say what you want to say in a way that sounds like it came from the real you.

My Mother Knew the Answers

Almost every day of her adult life, my mother wrote a letter to her mother in Ohio. I would ask, "What are you telling her today that you didn't already tell her yesterday?" Sometimes she showed me the letters, which were several typed pages long and invariably delightful. Like the *Seinfeld* show—always described as "a show about nothing"—they were usually about inconsequential texture-of-life things: how my father had missed his train, how the dog was under the kitchen table snoring like a drunken sailor, how I'd learned in school that day that the French word for lawyer is the same as the word for avocado.

If you'd asked me, back then, to write a three-page letter with so little news to report, I'd have been a blank. But my mother, who had been a prize-winning newspaper feature writer, sat there tapping away at a rapid clackety-clack on her red (she painted it) Royal typewriter, turning out those charming letters every day. I marveled at how effortlessly she did this, but now I understand it: She knew the answers to the fundamental writing questions I've been posing.

She knew her motivation and purpose and her audience of one. Her tone, her voice, her rhythm, and humor; her eye for the right anecdote; her good reporting, levels of candor, disclosure, and language—all of this was well established, meaning that it did not need to be reinvented on a daily basis.

She never had writer's block, never stalled before starting, never hit false notes. She knew who she was. Her writing voice was honed to perfection. She wrote well, she wrote fast, and she enjoyed it. All she had to do was press the Start button and she'd be off and running on her daily letter.

If you read those letters, you knew her. It's a shame they are lost because I could have put them together with minimal editing to produce a wonderful autobiography. It's too late for that now, but I offer her example as an illustration of the benefits of finding your answers and solving the many writing questions you face. As you get through them, the struggle of writing turns into a pleasure.

WRITING IS HARD

I recall a college writing teacher saying book-writing is so hard that anyone who finishes a book, *even if it's terrible*, deserves a standing ovation.

Everyone knows writing is hard. But I don't think the difficulty stops anyone who is seriously interested in trying to write. It's estimated that *fourteen million* American adults engage in some sort of creative writing every year. People *love* to write; some people *live* to write; very few of them are masochists who write because they love misery or can't get enough frustration.

Some problems, including the notorious writer's block, can be outwitted; others require struggling. The problems that are most likely to be terminal tend to happen early, at the very beginning or soon thereafter, but hazards are everywhere. The desire to quit is common and recurs on a weekly, daily, or even hourly basis.

So how do we deal with the guaranteed difficulty of writing?

I think what you should say to yourself is this: "Look, I know this is going to be hard, so I won't be shocked or confounded when trouble strikes. I'll understand *why* writing is hard, and I'll be ready for it, thanks to some proven wisdom and simple tactics that writers have been following forever. Writing my autobiography is a good thing to do; forget about giving up."

UNDERSTAND WHY WRITING IS HARD

Cure yourself of the common delusion that you are the sole victim of the difficulty of writing. It's not just hard for you, it's hard for *everyone*.

Thomas Mann said, "A writer is somebody for whom writing is more difficult than it is for other people." It should encourage the rest of us that a winner of the Nobel Prize in Literature complained about the difficulty of writing.

Another great quotation comes from E.B. White, who wrote *New Yorker* articles and children's books with a seemingly easy grace that is the envy of all writers. He made the ultimate statement on the frustration of writing, "When you say something, make sure you have said it. The chances of your having said it are only fair."

If the chances were only fair for the great E.B. White, what are the chances for you or me?

Why is writing so hard? *Talking* doesn't seem so hard, and it's clearly a close cousin to writing. We just signal our lips to start forming words, and out they come. Writing is often the opposite: We press the start button, and either nothing comes out or something jumbled and incoherent comes out.

Talking and writing might be cousins, but they are cousins many times removed. There are many substantial distinctions between them, but just in terms of *difficulty*, you should understand that the standards are different, the content is different, the values are different, and the forgiveness of sloppiness or inarticulateness is enormously different. Writing is *examined* while most talking is usually not. You can run your mouth and never make a point while talking, but in print it *shows*, badly.

The key difference between writing for the ear and the eye is that while most of us have acquired the full arsenal of talking, we have *not* acquired the writer's ability to translate these assets into print.

A good example is the sarcastic remark. In conversation, we deliver sarcasm with extreme sophistication, an intuitive multimedia mix involving tone of voice, facial expression, posture, signals of hostility and humor, all the elements and controlled inflections that an actor would blend into a perfect delivery of the line. But try that same remark in print, and all those aids are gone, and the same words might have a different effect, a puzzling effect, a backfiring effect, or no effect at all.

Here's another huge element regarding the difficulty of writing: It's not just about saying a lot of words, *it's about defining reality*. There is no established reality until someone defines it in language. A journalist goes to a scene of a battle and finds horrifying chaos—his job is to impose order and meaning, writing what's been called "the first draft of history," which is also the first draft of reality, telling who won, how many soldiers died, what caused the battle to unfold as it did, what are the key details. His interpretation becomes the definition of the battle's reality.

Subsequent "drafts" by others might modify or dispute that definition, and the defining process might go

YOU DON'T HAVE TO BE FAMOUS

on for centuries. But it *starts* with the first words. In your autobiography, when you describe your first dance or first baseball game, you're defining the reality of the experience. That's a lot more than just chattering about it.

Seen from this angle, the writer's task is formidable. It's about constructing or extracting *meanings* that didn't exist until you defined them. The miracle is that it's doable, and by you.

At first you were struggling just to express a clear idea in a single sentence; now you've climbed the ladder to the point where you're creating meanings. With each new level of difficulty, you're also reaching new levels of potential. When you write autobiography, you are *defining* your life. That's a big goal. Don't expect to achieve it without a struggle.

BALANCE FEAR WITH KNOWLEDGE

There is a tremendous amount of ego on the line when you're writing, and that means tremendous vulnerability. A writer needs to maintain a secure, or even inflated, ego to balance the fear of failure or inadequacy, but the writing process often seems like a conspiracy to break your confidence.

People take writing very personally. They approach it as a test and then make the test as unfair to themselves as possible, working under self-created tension that makes a positive outcome unlikely. The inevitably disappointing results are interpreted as irrefutable evidence that they are unequipped to write. This is mortifying and creates a feeling that a painful personal deficiency has been exposed to the entire world.

Irrational and wrong as this is, it is strongly felt. While a small number of non-writers suspend all self-criticism and assume that their work is marvelous because *they* wrote it, the majority lean in the opposite direction: Because they wrote it, it must be mediocre. I suspect that this verdict is less about their prose than their excessive readiness to confirm their worst fears: They desire to be quickly slain and carried from the battlefield rather than enduring any further humiliation.

What fear causes them to overlook is the all-important and obvious fact that (except in rare cases) writing is not just a talent, it is also *an acquired skill*. Failure to have acquired this skill is no more a personal deficiency than failure to have mastered riding a unicycle. A bad first try at writing is no more surprising than the disaster you would experience if you tried figure skating at the Olympics after not having skated since you were nine years old.

Most of the things that writers do are *learnable*. Norman Mailer has compared learning to write to learning to play piano—it takes a few years of focused study and practice until you can perform at a satisfactory level.

Satisfactory is all you need, and you've been doing some degree of writing for a long time, so we can skip the three years of study and practice. Remember now that you have rejected the fantasy of literary glory. All you want and need is enough ability to write your book in a way that serves your purposes—you don't have to write like a master.

No matter how well you write, self-doubt always hovers over a writing project. I think this is inherent in being exposed to judgment and self-judgment, as writers always are. The quality of their work is there for *anyone* to find fault with. Writers submitting their work to scrutiny hold their breath, waiting for the hammer blow of criticism.

There is a lot of tension in the writing process. It's reflected in the choke-up at the starting line (writer's block) and in the amazing ability of writers to find ways to stall when writing time rolls around. For nonwriters, it's often reflected in angry accusations directed at their high school English teachers, who, they say, quashed their natural writing potential by smothering them with rules of grammar, syntax, and punctuation and embarrassing vocabulary tests, which revealed their ignorance of words like *asseverate* or *adventitious* (words which are never used in written or spoken language and exist only in vocabulary tests).

Blaming gerunds and dangling participles for your writing woes is a feeble excuse when there are much better reasons for writing breakdowns, namely the two reasons I'm discussing here.

Reason #1 is that writing *does* create insecurity, doubt, tension, and even fear—for which your best preparation is simply being aware of them, knowing that they are in the cards as part of the writing experience. You can't negate them entirely, but you can deflate their impact by not being surprised or traumatized when they hit.

Reason #2 is that writing *is* hard. But a satisfactory level of writing skill is something you can acquire. It's not unattainable. If you want to do it and work at it, you'll be thrilled at how well you can do.

OUTSMART WRITER'S BLOCK

Being stuck at the start creates a special kind of frustration. Before you can even get going, you are tangled in knots, immobilized, virtually paralyzed. Your skills and bright ideas desert you like rats realizing they're about to go to sea on a leaky ship. Suddenly you cannot write a single respectable sentence or sustain the simplest chain of thought. Then it gets worse.

After a very short dose of this, you're ready to throw up your hands and quit. Many writing projects grind to a halt before the end of the third paragraph. The third paragraph often has a Bermuda Triangle effect—you go into it but never come out. And of course many writing projects don't even make it to the first *sentence*, as the writer wilts under the pressure and cannot get down even those first few words.

Welcome to writer's block.

I think of writer's block as a drooling, grinning monster that lurks at the starting line, waiting to pounce on unwary writers who either have *no* starting idea (the plan is to babble aimlessly until something develops) or an undisciplined *excess* of ideas (which behave like the proverbial army of cats: unmanageable and scampering off in every direction).

Here's what I advise. If you're bogged down at the beginning and feel the fangs of writer's block digging into you, take decisive emergency action, starting with defensive moves.

First, retreat. Break this bad spell. Don't sit there letting frustration boil over. Get up, shake it off, and go away for a while. Come back later when your mind is cleared and you're ready to try again.

Second, delete everything that's been contaminated by the writer's block virus. You'll recognize the difference between a start that's just not very good yet and a writer's block start that is so convoluted and hopeless that it seems to be pulling you down in quicksand. These bad starts are lethal and have to be gotten rid of, even if you invested

YOU DON'T HAVE TO BE FAMOUS

long hours or days working on them. Don't try to salvage anything from them, or you'll risk salvaging the problems that caused them.

Third, make a rule that until you get past this struggling phase, you will only write short sentences. Short sentences force you to deal in clear ideas. They force you to be concrete instead of abstract. It is hard to get lost in short sentences.

Some writers insist that writer's block does not exist. They think this, I suspect, because they are the lucky ones who have never been abandoned by their ability to do the single thing you must do to beat writer's block: Blast over the starting line without hesitation and drive hard through a few decent pages before stopping for air.

The way to outsmart writer's block is to begin with sure-thing momentum and get past the start so fast that it cannot get you in its clutches. You were vulnerable to writer's block because you were *not ready*. Now, be ready with a specific plan for the first pages.

Pick something you know you can write without bogging down. It can be an anecdote, an image, a scene, a memory, a moment, a description, a joke, a declaration— *anything that gets you moving.*

Before long, probably without realizing it, your writing muscles will loosen, the sun will come out, you'll relax into a natural writing rhythm, and there'll be no more danger of becoming road kill for writer's block. You'll be on your way to the relatively safe and straightforward territory of the middle.

"GET IT DOWN, THEN GET IT RIGHT"

Suspend self-criticism when you're trying to get started. Don't nitpick your own work. Don't sit there getting upset because what you're writing isn't instant perfection. Just write. *Get it down, then get it right.*

This is essential advice—practical advice with a psychological component. It is usually attributed to Ernest Hemingway, but he was surely not the first to realize that writing is almost always done in two steps: First you get something down on paper, *then* you go back and work on getting it right, through the process of rewriting.

(The word *rewrite* sometimes alarms inexperienced writers who think it means throwing everything out and doing it all over again. It's seldom that drastic. Think of it as a synonym for *revise*. It means going over your work many times—it might seem like five million times, but it's probably less—each time making changes, which might be tiny or significant. I would guess that 75 percent of the time you put into your book will be spent on rewriting. Rewriting is really the difference between a slapdash effort and a book you can really be proud of. I devote all of chapter thirteen to rewriting.)

A good start breaks the invisible writer's block barrier and generates words, which are blessedly tangible in comparison with the great nothingness that exists before anything is actually written. Once you've got a bunch of words, you have something to work with. This is a big step forward from having nothing but a blank page.

It's very important to understand that you will seldom get it down *and* right at the same time. This means the quality you'd hoped for in your first try is *almost never* going to be there. Quitting in despair is common as you survey your disappointing first efforts, but it's a mistake you will regret.

YOU DON'T HAVE TO BE FAMOUS

A reason why writing projects often meet such quick defeat is that inexperienced writers are too quick to declare their work inadequate, and the reason they do this is largely because they don't understand that rewriting will save the day, transforming hopeless pages into good pages. The reason they don't see this is that writers keep rewriting secret, erasing the clues to all the struggles they had and to how much hard labor it took to fight through their bad early writing and get it right. It is a matter of pride and skill to create an impression that the whole thing issued forth in a single natural flow.

This deception misleads the nonprofessionals into thinking that real writers can do it in one take. Since the nonprofessionals *can't* do that, they conclude that they are not real writers. But if they listened a little closer, they might hear good writers admitting that their brilliance took a lot of work. Somewhere I read an amusing line from the economist John Kenneth Galbraith, a marvelously clear and enjoyable writer, who recalled, "It was usually on about the fourth or fifth day [of rewriting] that I put in that note of spontaneity for which I am known."

Literary mystique also contributes to the notion that writers should achieve perfect composition on the first try. I have seen photographs and museum exhibits of manuscript pages written by legendary authors, with only a few cross-outs or word changes. The implication is that you are seeing a first and only draft, and that the rewriting amounted to nothing more than proofreading.

This is intimidating and might send the aspiring writer reeling with a sense of inferiority. But I don't buy it for a minute. True, certain geniuses have had bursts of inspiration when words and ideas rushed out fully formed, and all writers eagerly await their few short moments of glorious inspiration. But this sort of gift from the gods should be regarded as rare and certainly not sustainable in the grueling process of writing a book.

So, understand that the quality of your first tries will be *miles* from what you are hoping for. Don't make harsh or final judgments on yourself this early.

Don't Show It Around

Don't let other people read your work in its early stage. The odds are very strong that it's not ready: Your thoughts and goals haven't come together yet, and your prose is not fit to be read by anyone but you. If you're fishing for compliments, you probably don't deserve them yet. And at your vulnerable early stage, even gentle criticism might feel like being hit by a truck.

What's more, most amateur readers lack both diagnostic skill and the knack for dealing with sensitive writers (all writers are sensitive writers). In addition to inflicting emotional pain, they can give disastrously wrong, capricious, or careless advice, and you might not have enough confidence yet to ignore them.

Keep in mind that most readers, even those who are biased heavily in your favor, cannot look at a creative work in progress and see what it's *going* to be. They can only see what it is *now*, and a judgment (even a facial expression) on what it is *now* is not going to do your confidence any good. If you feel you must have feedback, ask for it *only* from people who know about writing—teachers, editors, or other writers—and no matter how much you respect them, don't let them overinfluence you.

I've always felt that the minute you let anyone read something you've written, your relationship with it changes. You no longer own it quite so privately or exclusively; its direction and evolution are no longer solely in your hands. Instead, you're negotiating with someone else's viewpoint or instincts. Even if that person is the best editor on the face of the Earth, he or she isn't *you*.

SOLITARY WRITING VERSUS GROUP WRITING

In chapter one, I said that while writing is ultimately a solitary pursuit, a lot of people like to come in from the cold of working alone and seek the company of groups—either in writing classes, memoir clubs, or working with partners or professional editors or mentors.

While working in groups has proven to be positive and even essential for many people, I'm not so sure it makes sense for autobiography. In this book, we are talking about a private book for your family, not an audience of outsiders (for which the class or club is the surrogate). This is different from the usual classroom focus; it seems to me that a private book should be written privately.

But maybe this is just a personal bias. I would want to write *my* autobiography by myself—it's a journey into *my* life, and, unfashionable as it may sound, I don't want to share the navigation. I also believe that too many cooks spoil the broth, and if something as important as my autobiography is going to be spoiled, I want to do it all by myself.

Maybe near the end of the writing it would be good to seek an objective opinion from a trusted friend, but that's as far as I would go in inviting other nonprofessionals to influence what and how I write.

That said, I'm also a proponent of doing anything that helps you succeed. If a class, club, or partner is what you need to get started, fine, but remember that at some point, you will have to fly on your own, without the support group.

As for writing classes, I took many in college and profited greatly. I've also taught writing classes, and the teaching experience is valuable, too.

Memoir clubs have been around for years and are quite popular now. You can probably find one by searching on the Internet. They are similar to college or post-college creative writing classes. Usually there is a teacher or leader and a small number of writers. The teacher offers some guidance; the group members hand in chapters which are read aloud to the group (or distributed in advance by e-mail) and critiqued.

Reactions range from valuable to confusing, and group chemistry inevitably plays a role, which might be positive or negative. You are at the mercy of your fellow writers—if your classmates are sensitive and perceptive, they might be extraordinarily helpful, but a bad group can do a world of damage. The same is true for your teacher, whose job is to provide wise opinion and guidance while preventing chaos or seriously wounded feelings.

The popularity of memoir-writing has also spawned a lot of services you can find on the Internet. You can hire people to help you write, link you to writing self-help groups or workshops, and help you self-publish. You can hire someone to interview you by phone and write the book for you or record your interviews and publish an "oral history." This can get expensive—I've seen prices ranging from a few thousand to $80,000. I have no idea of the professional quality or reliability of these outfits, but they're available. Of course, all of these services are a long distance from the original idea of writing a modest autobiography for a small circle of family and friends.

YOU DON'T HAVE TO BE FAMOUS

As for writing with a partner, your partner for autobiography writing would ideally be someone who's been in your life for many years, a spouse or a relative or an old friend. You would have to face many decisions, such as whether you would write separate books or a co-autobiography—the story of your family, marriage, or friendship. Would you have different roles in the process (one writes, the other edits or does research) or would you share the writing? If you both write, do you work on the same material or write alternating chapters? What happens if one of you wants to work on a strict schedule while the other wants a loose schedule? How do you arbitrate when you have disagreements? Who has final approval? How do you handle writing about each other?

The upside of cowriting a book is that you keep each other going, refreshing each other's optimism and energy levels, and making it harder to bog down or quit. These are good things, but group writing inevitably involves compromises, and pretty soon it's not *your* book any more. So if that's important, be careful.

Writing is hard, and multiple authors often make it even more complicated. Some people just cannot work together, and the result is feuding and damaged relationships and, very likely, an aborted project.

I've written two books with partners and bailed out of at least three opportunities to cowrite books because I sensed that the partnerships would not work. Looking back, I think I made the right decisions. Of the two successful partnerships, one worked because we had a clear-cut division of labor: He was the expert (a paleontologist and authority on the Galapagos), and I was the prose provider. The other book entailed zero division of labor—our skills, styles, and attitudes were substantially identical. We were longtime friends and had a great time writing a comic novel together, but we had no discipline, loved everything we wrote, and cut very little. It was an excellent learning experience, but the book was out of control. It was published, but no one took it seriously.

Of course, the ultimate risk of group writing is multiple voice and multiple viewpoints resulting in the mishmash known as "committee writing." One of the great quotations, usually attributed to the architect Frank Lloyd Wright, is "A camel is a horse designed by a committee." You don't want your book to be a gawky thing with humps. My advice would be not to risk it.

8

SET YOUR IMAGINATION FREE

Creativity can be discussed at great depth, length, and pomposity, but the simple version is that creativity is a form of play, a rebellion or escape from an adult mentality. Its motivating impulse is a childlike desire to set the imagination free.

Think of a bunch of kindergarten kids giddily slapping paint on sheets of butcher paper. Ask these kids to draw a dinosaur, and they do it in a few joyous, spontaneous strokes. You might not recognize the dinosaur, but they do.

As we grow up, we become inhibited and self-conscious about creativity and try to confine it to a narrow and practical range, doing carpentry or designing a garden. Adults who give signs of being creatively ambitious are thought to be suffering from delusions of grandeur, requiring swift mockery or put-downs (to their faces or behind their backs).

You might get a taste of this when word gets out that you're writing your autobiography. *The New York Times* columnist Maureen Dowd, in an obituary of her mother, recalled that "When I told her I was thinking of writing a memoir, she dryly remarked, 'Of whom?' "

Well, too bad about what other people think. You've chosen to give yourself a chance to enjoy creativity. A large part of the fun you'll get from writing will be the pleasure of releasing your imagination (and memory). Your best work will come out of these moments when you rise a little above your everyday self and into something much more interesting. So don't stifle your own instincts or ideas. To get the most out of your writing experience, trust your imagination, and when it seems to be leading you somewhere, follow it.

Let's talk now about getting yourself into a winning spirit as you take on the challenges of writing.

BE AUDACIOUS

Audacity is a soaring, liberating, defiant virtue. It smashes a pie in the face of that hand-wringing adult self that seems to be peering over your shoulder, issuing anxious warnings: "You can't say that. Where did this come from? Where are you going with that? This is so over-the-top and out of left field. You'll be embarrassed by this when you read it back."

I associate audacity with the combat pilots I knew when I was a navy information officer on aircraft carriers in Vietnam. I had always thought of courage in terms of facing danger and overcoming fear, but (unless I was fooled by their bravado) fear was not really a problem for these pilots.

They were brash and cocky and eager to tangle. They were undaunted speedsters who considered themselves invulnerable. They complained that a mission was boring if they had *not* been shot at by antiaircraft fire and surface-to-air missiles.

It was an article of faith among combat pilots that audacity (stopping short of recklessness) kept them alive. Attacking boldly is safer than flying scared. Flying with other audacious pilots is better than flying with an indecisive Nervous Nellie whose mind is on playing it safe.

Combat pilots are profligate spenders of audacity, and sooner or later their tanks would run low. A pilot would start being rattled by close calls. He would start losing confidence, and this was dangerous for the pilot himself and for his flying partners. The pilot would be taken out of combat duty for a few days and sent off to some rest and recreation venue, preferably Hong Kong, where he would be expected to party with rambunctious zeal and do everything possible to replenish his flyboy swagger.

It might seem like a Walter Mitty fantasy to suggest that writers have something in common with swashbuckling aviators. I confess that I've never been pursued by surface-to-air missiles or bored because no one was shooting at me. But within the physically undangerous confines of writing, I think most people who sustain creative careers do possess an audacious or rebellious spirit. They go with their instincts, take chances, don't fear criticism or worry what people will think. They believe that risk taking will always be rewarding.

In a low-key way, I applied this idea in my work as a speechwriter. Corporations tend to be fearful environments where obedience (sometimes called "alignment") is expected. CEOs or their aides often gave me extensive guidance on what they wanted in their speeches, spelling out the corporate party line, telling me how to organize it, perhaps suggesting a few writing ideas of their own. It was unthinkable that I would disregard these marching orders.

But I did. Audacity had been drilled into me in my training as a writer, and there was no way I was going to smother it as a corporate player. My policy became: *The first draft is mine*. I would be realistic, but I would write the draft audaciously (though not recklessly), going with my best instincts even if they were far more adventurous or colorful that what the client had in mind. My premise was that if this was intolerable to the client, he could fire me, or I could tone it down (and maybe still end up with more audacity than he'd expected). The corollary of *The first draft is mine* was that *The second draft is his*.

I'm glad to report that this approach was vindicated time after time, and no one ever called me subversive. Not every client loved it, and I have been sternly reminded of the original instructions more than a few times. But in a high percentage of first draft experiences, clients were happily surprised by the audacious spirit. Sometimes they were thrilled by it, telling me they couldn't wait to deliver the speech. Put a bold draft in front of them, and they liked it. They'd never seen one before.

Audacity produces better results.

The key to audacity is giving yourself *permission*. It may be a surprising idea that you sometimes have to give permission *to yourself*, but this happens commonly in writing when your creative instinct challenges your conventional instinct.

I've just given you two examples. A reader could reasonably question the relevance of my recollections about navy pilots in Vietnam and corporate speechwriting in

YOU DON'T HAVE TO BE FAMOUS

a book about writing autobiographies. And the truth is, they weren't even on my mind when I started writing this chapter. *They came along, and I let them in.* I could have chased them off or shut the door on them or edited them out later. But I didn't, because I gave myself permission to follow these spontaneous tangents and see if I could incorporate them in a way that made my points more interesting, enjoyable, and persuasive, perhaps even richer and more memorable. And frankly, more *me*.

This qualifies as risk-taking writing, but I'm not trying to glamorize it: It is risk taking on a very mild level. When I urge you to set your imagination free in your early drafts, it is this mild degree of audacity I have in mind. Go for the gusto, but don't go crazy.

Giving yourself permission to pursue ideas, instincts, memories, or unclear directions is a big step in writing. It's not as easy as it sounds. The key is learning to relax.

GET INTO THE MAGIC ZONE

I live in a suburb and often take a commuter train into New York City. The ride takes forty to fifty minutes. Around the halfway point, I tend to look up from whatever I'm reading and gaze out the window, thinking of nothing in particular. The cell phone conversations going on around me stop annoying me and fade into background babble. The train rumbles and rolls along.

Then my mind starts whirring.

If a writing project is on my mind, I find myself thinking about it with a detached clarity in which the mind seems to relax and generously hand over secrets or solutions it had stubbornly withheld. I take out my ever-present index card and take notes before they slip away.

What is even better is when this happens while writing. I have a name for this: I call it *getting into the magic zone.*

You're sitting there writing with no sense that anything exceptional is happening. You're intensely focused and barely realize that the writing is going well. Then you begin to notice that it's going better than well. And soon you're thinking: Gee, this is really good. Is this *me* writing this? *Where is this coming from?*

You're working on a higher level but don't know how you got there. Your creative juices are pumping. Insights and perceptions that eluded you now present themselves with blazing clarity. Language pours out easily. Everything is going right. And it's fun. Athletes talk about "playing out of my mind." Gamblers call it "being on a roll."

There is a sense of *access* to something mysterious and wondrous. It's not *you*. This magic seems to bypass the usual you. Writers talk about a feeling that they're not writing, they're *transcribing*.

Henry Miller called it "the dictation."

Edmund Wilson said it seemed like the writing was coming not from his brain but from his right arm. He just watched it appear on paper.

Susan Sontag said writing often seemed to "come out of my fingers."

Henry Louis Gates said, "This book wrote itself. I would look at my pen and think, 'This is the smartest pen in all of Italy.'"

Norman Mailer said, "It's all there, a gift. You don't even seem to have much to do with it."

Saul Bellow said his novel *Augie March* just came to him, and all he had to do was "be there with buckets to catch it."

This is the stuff of great writing adventures, a far cry from the usual plodding struggle. You are aloft in the magic zone. You are dramatically better than the writer you usually are. But then—

—It shuts off.

You float back down to Earth, to your normal self. And you realize that the moment you became conscious of being in the zone was the moment you began to lose altitude.

Furthermore, your stay was so temporary. It doesn't seem fair. "The unconscious has done its job," says Norman Mailer. "It's damned if it's going to give you any more right now."

The magic zone experience is a small taste of what genius is all about. A genius has easier access to the magic zone and gets to stay there longer. You and I only get a momentary foot in the door, and our door is on a much lower floor. However, be thankful for this and grab what you can get. Our best prose, our best leaps forward, and most of our insights and inspirations are gifts from our whirl in the magic zone.

(It should be said as a caution that the zone experience is not 100 percent trustworthy. Sometimes it's illusory. You come back the next day to savor the results of yesterday's grand flight, but it turns out to be disappointing or even incomprehensible, as if you'd been taking LSD. But most of the time, the results are notably better than your average work.)

Some writers scoff at the idea of the magic zone or "dictation" from a mysterious source, perhaps because they attribute their best performance to hard work and professionalism and don't want a hocus-pocus concept like magic stealing any of the credit. I respect that opinion, and I'm sure I would share it if I hadn't had the same kind of experience the writers I've just quoted have described. However, the space between believing and not believing in a certain kind of creative magic might not be as great as it seems.

I don't think you get a free ticket to the magic zone: You don't get in simply by knocking on the door. Many of the attributes of professionalism are prerequisites for magic zone admittance. You have to put in the time. You have to concentrate and be prepared and know what you're talking about. You have to relax, and you have to give yourself permission to set your mind free. And you will not get into the magic zone without audacity. There is no admittance for the timid.

Three Moments to Look Forward To

The magic zone experience is the best part of the writing experience, but I can think of three other very good moments.

- **Getting over the opening hump:** The ice is broken on the start; you're off and running.

- **Entering the home stretch of the first draft:** This is the beginning of the transition between clawing away desperately and finally being in control, as if a power struggle has finally shifted in your favor. The challenge is far from ended, but you realize that you're going to whip this beast.

- **The start of rewriting:** Your first draft is finished; it's now time to go back over everything and get it right. Tension decreases.

Finishing the book, in my experience, is never the champagne occasion I expected. The moment you declare your book done, the whole experience enters the past tense. Your future seems bleak without the book to work on. You face a version of postnatal depression.

However, by the next day, things brighten up. You have a day without writing—and what a guilt-free pleasure it is. You also realize that you not only endured the rigors of the book-writing marathon, but you made it to the finish line. That makes you a winner.

THE WAIVER

The notion that the writing police are keeping an eagle eye on what you write is, of course, ridiculous. So is the notion that you need permission to audaciously free your imagination. You make the rules here. You are the boss of this book.

This is your reward for giving up hope of publishing fame and fortune—you don't need to play by the rules of that game. Instead, you have what I call the "It's *your* book waiver."

The waiver gives you the option of waving good-bye to all the constraints and disciplines normally imposed on book writers. You do not have to accept the professional judgment of any editor. No publisher can order you to do things a certain way "because that's what sells." To whatever degree you choose, you are exempt from having to compete with professional writers or from abiding by any writing practices or doctrines you don't like. You can write and design your book any way you want. It's *yours*.

You have a freedom that professional writers never experience. There is no one whose approval you need, no one crossing out your favorite sentences or setting deadlines or telling you that what you've written has to be "tweaked" or changed to suit the tastes of people you don't even know.

Your freedom is nearly total, although I would advise against libeling people or accusing them of crimes or conduct that might provoke lawsuits or other repercussions.

I'll also suggest some caveats on the important issue of how you write about events of great sensitivity to others. Otherwise, you are the final authority. You are moving into a boss-free universe.

What are you going to do with this freedom? As much as we want freedom, we also want boundaries. We might want final responsibility to be someone else's, or at least shared. But the waiver doesn't mean you *must* sail off on your own and operate with no guidance or discipline. It only says that the decision on how much creative freedom you exercise is up to you.

Let's consider the range of options.

One option is to go wild, breaking the rules with abandon, fabricating new versions of reality, being reckless or shocking or consistently referring to your brother-in-law as "The Shithead."

The waiver permits these liberties but makes discipline *your* responsibility. You can diverge from accepted standards of good writing at any time, but you should think twice (at least twice) about doing so if you are serious about your book.

Going in markedly idiosyncratic directions could be good (showing your unique personality and style) or bad (annoying readers with tiresome gimmicks). Writing experience teaches that excesses that make you smile today often make you wince tomorrow.

Also, keep in mind that climbing out too far on creative limbs tends to require virtuoso writing gifts, which

YOU DON'T HAVE TO BE FAMOUS

you might not possess. A Tom Wolfe or a Hunter Thompson can do it, but their imitators go down in flames.

Here's another waiver option: *Never* invoke it. Cut yourself no slack and try to write a book that meets professional or high-quality amateur standards and would be appropriate for publication in the real world.

This is an admirable course. A strong argument in its favor is that the more you allow yourself to wander from the straight and narrow of standard book-writing values—from prose discipline to selection of content—the more you risk experiments that might backfire. Instead, play it safe and orthodox.

This does not rule out creative or personalized approaches. Your autobiography is a personal document by definition, and it *should* have a "my-way" feel. Among other things, the waiver frees you from an autobiographical formula that might be suitable for a former secretary of state but is too highly starched for you. And as I suggested in chapter four, if you want to dispense with the standard chronological model and use a different structure, you're free to do that.

But there is a middle ground between permissive and strict, and it's what I recommend.

First, be aware that you have the waiver. Appreciate that it relieves some pressure to conform to guidelines or expectations that aren't right for you. You're allowed to be *you*, and the more *you* the better.

Second, write and structure the book the way you want. Its style should reflect your character and your story. Ignore what you think you're *supposed* to do and do what feels right. Make sure to let it evolve as you go along. If it's not working, back up and rethink.

Third, keep the waiver in reserve and don't use it *until you need it*, in big ways or small. There may be parts of the book you simply cannot write or don't want to write. They might be too emotional, too painful, or too hurtful to others. Or maybe you just plain can't remember the details.

Don't get into a habit of using the waiver to evade challenges (especially the fundamental challenges of formal writing), but if your judgment tells you to exclude something, do it. By the same token, if there's something you want to include but have doubts about, you can give yourself permission to ignore those doubts and go with your best instincts. If you think readers will notice that you've excluded something significant or included something risky, it might be good to tell why you decided as you did. Unless you'd rather not. You don't have to justify your decisions to anyone but yourself.

TELL THE TRUTH

Setting your imagination free and enjoying your wide latitude under the waiver permit an extraordinarily unhindered writing opportunity, but there is one limit: You have to tell the truth. You cannot play games with the truth, stretch the truth, or alter the truth in your favor.

Yes, the waiver allows some pulling of punches to avoid hurting people, and we all know that a "whole truth and nothing but the truth" policy is often just an excuse for saying things that are blunt and cruel. We humans are sensitive creatures, easily wounded by the smallest slights, but being wounded *in print* is especially painful because it seems so permanent and public.

Omitting can be a form of lying. In a book about a public figure there would have to be an exceptionally strong argument to justify omissions on the grounds of protecting feelings, but I think we can permit a little leeway for an unfamous person writing a private autobiography.

However, being *too* positive also raises an honesty issue. Sugarcoating is a temptation that many autobiographers find hard to resist. In the warm glow of nostalgia, they forget or forgive all the blows and betrayals and defeats and disappointments and grievances of life. Instead, they skirt all forms of unpleasantness and adopt a speak-no-evil policy, putting an upbeat spin on everything, finding silver linings everywhere, and making rose-colored glasses part of the daily writing uniform.

At first this is simply bland and boring. Then it gets worse. While the motivation for sugarcoating might be good-hearted and well-meant, the reader figures out that an everything-is-great interpretation is being imposed on everything. All conflict is being censored out, all negatives are being papered over or omitted, and the result is as inauthentic as propaganda. Truth has become secondary. Reality has been altered—and that's lying.

You might be reading this and thinking that a warning about truth doesn't apply to you because there are no lies you'd be tempted to tell. But (as an old saying goes) the truth is seldom pure and never simple. I guarantee that you will find yourself in gray areas, facing surprisingly difficult judgments. Truth can be evasive, puzzling, hard to separate from opinion, or even unknowable. Objectivity can be difficult, if not impossible, and memory can be highly unreliable.

As an autobiographer, you must be acutely aware of the trickiness of truth issues. Especially when you are discussing your own behavior, it is human nature to see what you want to see and tilt judgments in your favor. And, of course, some people tilt in the *other* direction: They are too willing to blame themselves and absolve others, too convinced that everything was their fault.

The risk with revising history is that what might start out as a single instance of mild truth stretching escalates into a pattern of lying. You, as the writer, must realize that this is a malignancy that cannot be tolerated because it destroys your credibility and the trustworthiness of your book, violating your unwritten contract with readers.

So it is essential to commit to truth telling wholeheartedly. You don't have to tell *everything* but you should give serious thought to anything that misrepresents what really happened. You have to cultivate an instinct for recognizing truth and a hound dog's nose for your own falseness. Police yourself like a veteran detective whose operating premise is that everyone is lying. If you don't, you'll feel guilty about what you've written, and even if you don't feel guilty, readers will probably smell the rat.

So don't just be honest, be *conspicuously* honest. Demonstrate consistently that you are keenly aware of honesty issues and committed to a scrupulous standard of credibility.

As I said earlier, if you don't remember something or have doubts about what happened or just don't want to discuss it, all you have to do is say so openly. If you're guessing or speculating or wondering, say so. If you're using facts that others might dispute, acknowledge that the facts are in question.

If you're reconstructing a conversation or an incident, make sure the reader understands that you're only speculating. Readers will give you latitude on approximating

YOU DON'T HAVE TO BE FAMOUS

things that were said or done a long time ago, but don't stretch it any further than necessary.

Don't use quotes or information from unidentified sources ("A certain member of the family—I can't say who—told me that ...") because quotations from unidentified speakers raise well-founded suspicions that the writer is making things up.

Don't try to sweep things under the rug or get away with anything. Don't slant facts to show how badly you were treated or to avenge old slights or grievances. These are cheap motives, and they will drag you down.

This is your book, maybe the only one you will ever write, and it is your written legacy. Don't tarnish its integrity with anything false.

Spread your wings and fly, but don't cheat.

STRATEGIES FOR
A GOOD START

Figuring out how to start is a rare challenge in which it would be desirable to put the cart before the horse. If you could just get a good look at that cart, you would have a much better idea of how to design the right horse.

It is a built-in frustration of writing that it's hard to tailor a start for a book that hasn't been written yet. How can you create the ideal foundation before you've really figured out the structure? How can you introduce the character and direction of the book before its character and direction have emerged?

It's often said that there are a million ways to tell a story—and thus a million ways to start one (and everything I say about starting applies not only to beginning your book but also to chapters, sections, even paragraphs and sentences). Sometimes an obvious and conventional starting idea presents itself and you should seize it—at least for now—but this is a moment when the creative window is wide open. There are infinite possibilities and the right choice will make a difference, giving you a boost in energy and allowing all your material to fall neatly into place. While I've warned against uncertainty and bogging down at the starting line (an invitation to writer's block), it's worth living dangerously for a brief period while you try to get lucky with an unexpected idea.

But how do you do this? How do you generate a good starting idea?

First, you need a menu—you need to be aware of your choices. Ask yourself this question: "Other than a chronological start, what *other* ways of starting can I think of?"

Just posing this question will get your creative wheels turning. You'll think of different aspects of the subject you want to write about and judge each of them as a possible starting point. You'll realize there are many ways to begin, each of them with a different way of structuring and shaping everything to follow. Later in this chapter, I'll describe several "angles of approach" for starting and leave it to you to consider the most attractive candidates.

But how do you distinguish a promising idea from a going-nowhere idea? As you consider your menu of possible starts, what makes one idea pop out as the right choice? The answer is that you have to have a sense of what you *want* from your start so you can recognize the potential of an idea and instinctively want to try to make it work. Let's consider the ingredients of a good start.

WHAT MAKES A GOOD START GOOD?

I'm going to suggest five objectives of a good start. You might not achieve all five objectives in your first few paragraphs but a good start leads you nicely to all the things you need to accomplish. And remember that you will spend a lot of time polishing and rewriting the start so don't panic if it doesn't achieve all these objectives in your first try.

1. Engage readers quickly and aggressively. Over time, what holds readers is value and character, but first you need *the hook*, the promise that causes them to read the next paragraph and then the paragraph after that until you've won them over, and they decide to stay.

Sweep them up in a good story or compelling situation. Physical action is a traditional solution, but a slam-bang action scene is not required as long as you create some sort of initial momentum and energy. And you have to be able to sustain it without a sharp drop-off. Three pages of lively storytelling that comes to a dead stop as you gear down into slow-moving narrative is not really a start, it's a stunt. The interest it creates will be short-lived.

In an autobiography, your hook might be as low-key as a demonstration that this book or chapter will be a worthwhile reading experience. It might suggest a revelation of unknown or fascinating material, a strong emotion or interesting situation, a surprising insight into the author (meaning you), or something relating directly to the reader (e.g., talking about your children *to* your children).

2. Demonstrate that you know what you're doing and where you're going. Make it clear you know your job is to *deliver* and that you're going to do it without asking the reader to be patient as you flail around trying to get on track. Convince readers that they're in good hands with you as the writer and that you are taking them in a clear and certain direction.

It's important to project confidence and command of content and voice. Give no hints that you don't know what you're doing.

3. Establish a good conversation with the reader. Kurt Vonnegut said you have to "be a good date for the reader." You have to create an immediate relationship that responds to basic questions about who you are and what it will be like to accompany you on this autobiographical journey. The real-life relationship you already have with family and friends reading the book will give you a head start but a writer-reader relationship must now be built on top of it.

Different kinds of books require different relationships between writer and reader. Autobiography probably requires a more personal and possibly more intimate relationship than any other kind of book. But this still leaves vast room for variation.

As I started working on this book, I decided it was my duty to read an autobiography often hailed as one of the greatest by an American, *Personal Memoirs of U.S. Grant*, first published in 1885. It is a long book, originally published in two volumes. I was not eager to confront that much detail on the Civil War, and my enthusiasm dropped even lower when I read the opening sentence, "My family is American, and has been for generations, in all its branches, direct and collateral."

This was hardly a dynamite start. Stylistically, it promised a dry and far too comprehensive account in a style that seemed too formal for a twenty-first-century reader. I flipped through the pages and saw nothing to convince me I was wrong. U.S. Grant appeared to be anything but a "good date for the reader." I did not look forward to a lengthy conversation with him and wondered why his book was so admired. If I hadn't already purchased the book, I would have put it back on the shelf.

But since I owned it, I gave it a try. And while my original assessment was not wrong, I discovered that before the end of the first chapter, I had developed an affection and respect for Grant. I'd intended to skim the book in an hour. I ended up reading every word.

I recommend Grant's first chapter because it shows that a high-powered, attention-grabbing blastoff is *not* necessary. His voice is businesslike but modest and utterly unaffected. He makes no effort to sell himself to the reader (of course, he didn't have to—he was a very famous man as a commander of victorious armies and a former president of the United States), and there is no apparent hook, *until* you realize that the hook is the quiet integrity of his character.

A twenty-first-century author might have opened with a spectacular battle scene or an historic sit-down with the opposing general, the Robert E. Lee of his times. But Grant, in what might be an inspiration to unfamous autobiographers, delays these high-impact scenes and hooks you instead with his *lack* of great-man ego. You understand right away that he will never glamorize himself or clamor for credit and that his account of events will not be distorted by vanity or self-interest. He closes the chapter with two self-deprecating childhood stories about making a fool of himself in horse trades. I didn't actually laugh at the stories (though I'd bet nineteenth-century readers roared at these homey, confessional anecdotes) but I liked him from that point on. It might have helped that he had some editing assistance from his publisher, Mark Twain.

Contrast Grant's start with Frank McCourt's opening of his 1996 best-selling memoir, *Angela's Ashes*:

> *My father and mother should have stayed in New York where they met and married and where I was born.... When I look back on my childhood, I wonder how I survived at all. It was, of course, a miserable childhood.... Worse than the ordinary miserable childhood is the miserable Irish childhood, and worse yet is the miserable Irish Catholic childhood....*

Wow. If U.S. Grant was holding it in, Frank McCourt was letting it all hang out.

These starts could hardly be more opposite, but both achieve the same goal: The authors establish their voices firmly and get their stories moving from their first words, convincing you of their integrity and competence, and telling you what kind of conversation is about to begin.

Thinking of autobiography as a (one-sided) conversation or "date" with readers leads to an interesting question: Is this conversation external or internal? That is, is your book the equivalent of sitting down in your living room and telling a small group of people the story of your life (external), or are you having an internal conversation with *yourself* while allowing readers to listen in?

This is a subtle but possibly important distinction. I'm not sure that your decision would be easily detectable in what you ultimately write, but it would certainly affect your point of view as you do the writing.

Are you addressing an audience or reflecting in private? If you are starting a story, let's say, about a childhood visit to your grandparents, is the goal to report the facts of the visit—a relatively descriptive or journalistic objective—or is it something more personal: digging down into memory to recapture a distant experience, discover something unseen at the time, or reflect on what it means to you today.

Of course, it could be all of the above, and the more the better. But whatever you do, your chances of success increase with your awareness. At some point in your start—though probably not in your first attempt to write it—you have to know your primary intent and signal it to the reader. If you do that, the reader will look forward to hearing more of what you have to say.

4. Lay a foundation. The start is not just the first thing you say, it's a foundation. The rest of the book or chapter will be built on it. So what you need is the beginning of a structure that can support what's to follow. You might not achieve this on the first page, but you should certainly put some sort of foundation in place near the beginning.

In addition to establishing the book's purpose and personality and making it compelling to readers, you have to start establishing whatever factual groundwork and scene setting will be needed to launch successive chapters or topics. As a check-off list, it might be helpful to make sure you're answering journalism's "Five Ws and H" questions: who, what, when, where, why, and how?

5. Excite the writer. If *you* aren't stimulated by the start, forget about stimulating anyone else. This is often overlooked as an objective of the start, but I think it's obviously essential that the writer is energized about continuing to write the story.

If there's a choice between doing what you think will please readers and doing what you want for yourself, please yourself. Doing it *your* way will stoke your ambition and creativity—trying to do it in what you think is *their* way will probably lead to a half-hearted effort. Be confident that if you do it your way and do it well, it will end up pleasing readers even if it isn't exactly what they had in mind.

All writers have had the experience of writing a start that simply refuses to come to life. You think, "This is just not happening. It's dead-on-arrival. I can't stand to write another word of this." There's no going on after this dreary signal registers in your mind. You can quit now or quit later. If you've written a start that leaves you bored or uncaring—even if it is otherwise defensible—don't try to fix it. Junk it and start all over with something else.

If there's a single quality that's critical to a good start, it's energy in any form. As you write, just keep asking yourself whether you're getting enough energy into your pages.

"It Is in the Beginnings and Endings That We Lie"

This observation, from the great Russian dramatist Anton Chekhov (who also wrote nearly six hundred short stories), is an exceptional insight about starting and finishing. Chekhov did not mean lying in the sense of outright dishonesty. He meant the artificiality or falseness we reveal when we have not yet gained command over our writing voice or story. Basically, we're faking it, getting something down long before we get it right.

This is a common problem in the early pages when there is so much for the writer to figure out and no way to do it other than working through a lot of untested notions, some of which are way off the mark. The problem subsides as we move into the more comfortable cruising voice of the middle pages. But then as we approach the ending, we become self-conscious and uncertain again, and the falseness returns.

The best way to cope with this is to recognize its predictability. Understand that you'll have to come back to the start many times before you get it right. The start will probably demand more rewriting than anything else in your book. So if you're having a Chekhovian crisis at the beginning (or end), and everything you write seems to ring false, just concentrate on getting something marginally adequate in place so you can move on. Don't compound your uncertainty by overreaching with something fancy or flashy, ending up with something so embarrassing that you can't bear to proceed. Make it as straightforward as possible. You'll improve it later.

E.B. White said, "To achieve style, begin by affecting none." The impulse of many inexperienced writers is to do the opposite, affecting style as hard as they can in hopes of stumbling onto something flamboyantly brilliant. But learn from Chekhov and think of affecting as pretending to be something you're not (i.e., lying).

This doesn't mean that "affecting none" is an easy alternative. It requires discipline and an eagle eye for spotting and then removing your excesses, artificialities, and false notes. Inexperienced writers often swing erratically from one tone of voice to another, as if they were trying on different personalities—they swerve from chatty to earnest to whimsical to deep thinking to distant to overwrought, and so on. These wrenching fluctuations are the lies and affectations that haunt their early pages and undermine their starts.

If it's in the beginnings and endings that we lie, it's in the middles where we finally relax and have a much easier time being authentic. This suggests a tactic: If you're really having trouble with the start, just find a quicker way to get to the middle. Maybe you can even do it on the first page.

Instead of carefully setting up a story, just dive into it. You might find later that the material you planned to use to lead into the story fits nicely as explanatory material *after* the story, when you're safely into the middle.

ANGLES OF ATTACK

A moderate amount of *unpredictability* often adds fresh energy as you hook your readers by signaling that you're using your imagination and not grinding out the book according to a template. The message is: You can't stop reading, this is going to be good.

Think of the start as an entrance and think of readers as your guests. You want to pull them in and get them involved as if you were giving a dinner party, orchestrating their arrival, their participation in predinner conversation or cocktails, the move to the table, the transition from appetizers to the main course and dessert, and perhaps a deeper or more entertaining level of conversation before the conclusion.

I've always discussed the start in terms of doors: front door or side door.

1. **Front door versus side door.** You can make a formal, orthodox entrance through the front door (U.S. Grant) or give the reader something unexpected by coming in through the side (Frank McCourt).

For autobiography on the chronological model, an opening like "I was born in Chevy Chase, Maryland, on May 5, 1955" is about as front door as it gets. The first benefit is that the reader recognizes the form and is immediately comfortable with it. The second is that the writer knows exactly what to do and where to go.

But as all journalists know, there are two ways of structuring a report.

The basic "hard news" story in a newspaper is *not* written with a beginning-middle-and-end structure. Instead of building toward an ending, it packs all the important information into a summary at the top, and then descends into lesser details. (This structure is usually described as an inverted pyramid with the lesser material at the bottom because cutting from the bottom is the way stories are trimmed to meet space requirements).

The second way to start a news story is with a "soft" or "feature" approach that circles in on the news-making event rather than making a beeline for it. "When Martin Smith reached into his pockets yesterday morning, he couldn't find enough money to pay for his bagel" is a soft lead, and the reader understands that the writer is beginning a story about Martin Smith's personal finances. "Martin Smith won the ten-million-dollar state lottery yesterday" is a hard lead with the basic fact of the news reported first: Someone named Martin Smith has won the lottery. We'll find out later that he couldn't afford breakfast.

The hard news or front-door approach is *direct*. You summarize main points, and then start backing them up with facts.

The soft news or side-door start reaches the main points *indirectly*, usually from a human interest angle and often involving storytelling. The storytelling either leads to the facts or, even better, attaches them along the way. Readers like this because they don't feel bombarded with data; they hardly realize how many facts they're absorbing.

The front-door approach is more about *telling;* the side door is about *showing*. Front door relies on facts; side door is more about offering something that gets the reader involved without knowing much about the story. Front door

YOU DON'T HAVE TO BE FAMOUS

is foolproof but possibly dull; side door is riskier—it takes a chance on catching the reader's imagination, but if it fails, it tests the reader's patience.

Front and side door are *both* good strategies, and you should consider both each time you start a new chapter. You might decide to vary your selection from chapter to chapter—front door for chapter one, side door for chapter two.

If a topic is intimidatingly large, and you're not ready to confront it head-on, back into it through the side door instead. Take some small sidelight just because it is interesting and easy to write. Start there and work your way toward the big central topic.

My Favorite "Side-Door" Start

Here's my favorite speechwriting experience involving a side-door start.

In 1991, I wrote a speech for a major Wall Street figure who wanted to deplore what was being called a "credit crunch," the reluctance of banks to lend start-up money to small entrepreneurs.

Economics topics tend to be heavy (sleep inducing), so I hunted around for a way to bring it to life. I ended up with a true story. It was about a young man from a poor background in Michigan in 1862. He saved a boy from being killed by a rolling railroad car. The boy's grateful father got the young man a job, training as a telegraph operator. The young man immediately demonstrated a remarkable gift for technology, and when he was twenty-nine, he decided to create what he called "an invention factory."

This required financing, but he was not an attractive candidate for a bank loan: He was ill groomed, hard of hearing (and disconcertingly loud of speech), had almost no formal education (his mother homeschooled him because his teachers thought he was "addled"), and an "invention factory" was an unheard-of idea.

Would this man have received bank financing in the credit-crunch atmosphere of 1991? Of course not. It was obvious that his loan request would be denied.

As the audience listened to this story and agreed with its conclusion, the speech then dropped a bomb: The young man in the story was none other than Thomas Edison, who was on his way to becoming America's greatest inventor. And he was not just a technology genius—he was also a businessman and entrepreneur who established a company that would become a colossus of the American economy, General Electric.

"Imagine the tragedy of Thomas Edison's incomparable contribution never materializing because he couldn't raise capital to get started," said the speaker. The speech went on from there, but the argument was already won. The side-door opening about Thomas Edison took only 482 words of a 5,229-word speech. It was the equivalent of a first round knockout.

---

2. **Shuffle the sequence.** What happens chronologically first is not necessarily the start, and what happens last is not necessarily where you should end.

Try this: Write down the most conventional outline you can imagine for a chapter you're about to begin or an event you're about to describe. Then take the beginning, middle, and end *and shuffle them*. Think about putting the apparent ending at the beginning (start with the day of your retirement rather than your first day on the job and then trace your career backward). Or skip the beginning and start with the middle ("After thirteen years, I suddenly could no longer tolerate corporate work and knew I wanted to

YOU DON'T HAVE TO BE FAMOUS

be a teacher"). Or consider putting a conventional opening at the end ("There were many good reasons to become an airline pilot, but when I think back to it now, I believe it all goes back to being a kid watching big jets high in the sky as they soared over my house at the beginning of their journeys across the ocean. I looked up at those planes and knew I wanted to devote my life to flying. And I did.")

If nothing else, this exercise will shake up your imagination and suggest creative permutations and options. Just as you might want to switch your starts from front door to side door (or vice versa), you also might tap into unexpected narrative energy by varying the predictable sequences of beginnings, middles, and ends.

3. Start later, end sooner. Again, what happens first need not be the start, and what happens last is not always the place to end. Think about getting into your stories *later* and out of them *sooner*. Instead of starting with step one ("As the school year ended the family decided to take a vacation to San Francisco."), start at step three ("None of us will ever forget the sight of clouds rushing in to completely conceal the Golden Gate Bridge."). This would relieve you of telling the pretrip story and get you right into the action in San Francisco. Any necessary pretrip material could be worked in as you go along. Of course, another option would be to start at step ten of the vacation story and work backwards ("I think our trip to San Francisco was the greatest vacation of my life.").

The same tip also works for endings. Instead of ending with step ten or even rattling on *beyond* step ten (the flight home, telling friends about the trip, subsequent visits to California, etc.), you could bring the story to a crisp conclusion before you even checked out of your San Francisco hotel (which might have been step eight: "We looked out our window at a San Francisco sunset and decided this was the most beautiful city in the world").

4. Start with your best material? Or build up to it? My years in television strongly influence my decision on this question. When you work in TV, you develop an awareness of viewers holding their remotes in their hands, ready to change channels the moment you cease to be interesting. You have to keep winning their attention moment by moment. You cannot afford a slow buildup toward your best material—by the time you get there, the audience might be gone.

Don't save your peak material. Start with it.

Okay, but *then* what do you do? Where do you go after you've played your biggest card? My answer is that peak material generates more peak material. *That's why it's peak material.* So start with your best story or even the best moment of the best story. Establish that as the level where you begin.

If the defining moment of your life took place when you were forty-five years old, *start there*—don't hold it until you've described the previous forty-four years, dragging the reader through parts of your life that even you don't care about. If you start with what's important, it will lead to telling why it was important and what it led to—so just follow that trail, and you'll be off to a good start. Work all the other stuff in along the way.

Finally, understand this about a good start: Readers will forget it. You put in all that work and creativity, maybe taking a gamble with something unconventional, but by the end of the chapter, it's falling off the edge of memory.

However, if the chapter succeeded, the launch should get much of the credit. That attention-catching angle of attack, that surprising reversal of predictable sequence, that side-door opening that cut right to the best material while jumping over details that might have been distracting drudgery—*that* was the source of the vitality that made the chapter good reading. Readers might forget it, but the writer will not.

10

TELLING STORIES

Stories are the building blocks of autobiography. People want to read them and writers want to write them—and they're probably what you write best. I hesitate to say stories are *easier* to write than anything else, but you might find this to be true.

Stories can be sagas or slices of life or moments frozen in time. They can be painful or poignant or playful, ordinary or extraordinary. They can be dramatically life changing or they can simply describe everyday life.

Ideally, your stories will be linked in some way, so they flow into or out of each other in a narrative that seems connected and coherent. But you might also find that the stories you want to tell do not have a natural connection.

For example, you might decide that a chapter on a certain period of your life should consist of three or four stories that are equally important but unrelated. Instead of forcing or fabricating transitions, the solution might be as simple as putting them in the same chapter and using a typographical symbol (such as *** or ###) to separate them and show that they stand apart.

In the interests of consistency, if you do this in one chapter, you should consider making it the chapter style throughout the book. A measured amount of variety and unpredictability is good, but format changes from chapter to chapter run the risk of creating a making-this-up-as-you-go-along feeling that will cost you respect from your readers.

DISCOVERING CAUSATION IN STORIES

Think imaginatively about how you organize or group your stories and be alert to how the sequence of stories can have surprising results. Putting stories side by side might expose patterns or themes you hadn't suspected.

For instance, a story about quitting a job might not reveal anything about you, but three such stories in a row might suggest that you've been a serial job quitter. A discovery like this will push you to examine your behavior and try to explain it. Perhaps you'd always attributed your job quitting to outward circumstances—bad bosses, inadequate pay, office politics, too much time away from the family. But now you see a pattern, and it leads you to understanding something about yourself that you'd never quite realized. It could be any of a number of things: You dislike authority, you don't like working, you can't put up with a boring job, you should have tried harder to get more challenging positions, you should have started your own business or gone a different way entirely.

What I am getting at here is a pursuit of *causation*. Can we look back at aspects of life we never fully understood and suddenly have new insight into why things happened as they did? A seemingly inconsequential story can take an unexpected turn and reveal causes that never occurred to us until this moment. This is the kind of "discovery" I've mentioned as one of the prime motivations for writing autobiography.

There are times in storytelling when it is inescapably incumbent on the writer to search for causes. If you describe a surprising change or event that raises obvious questions about its cause—let's say a sudden divorce or career change involving you or someone else—you have to find a way to explain it. If you don't know the answer, you have a choice between cautious and well-labeled speculation or simply admitting you don't know. But you must provide *something*—you cannot leave the reader with only a gaping hole where an explanation should be.

That said, it's necessary to seek a restrained balance between your writer's responsibility for eliciting causes and your best judgment of how far you can go in probing for causes without getting into destructive territory. Profound sensitivities might be involved, and the possibility of inflicting pain could be high—even if the thought you're expressing seems fairly harmless to you and certainly not meant to injure.

In a family, the smallest spark can set off volcanic emotions. I once witnessed a scene in my own family in which *a tone of voice* (interpreted as patronizing) created a breach between an aunt and uncle (both over seventy years old) that was not repaired for more than three years. I have some thoughts on the deep-seated emotion that caused such a minor offense to have such major consequences, but I would write about it with the greatest delicacy because I think we should keep ourselves on a tight leash when it comes to adventures in amateur psychoanalysis (although we have far more leeway in analyzing ourselves than in analyzing others).

You may have seen similar events in your own family. I'll say more about this later, but for now the lesson is: Write about causation with care and humility, and if instinct tells you to backpedal toward superficiality, do so. There are a lot of things worse than superficiality.

I think what writers love about stories is their all-purpose nature. You can use them as illustrations or examples, as sources of energy and momentum, as ways of showing things through action that you would have trouble telling through exposition.

And stories are excellent solutions for starting. If you're having trouble starting, I strongly recommend that you quickly reject ambitious approaches that aren't working and commence storytelling from the first word. You can come back later and wedge in preparatory or introductory material *before* the story, if you think that's a good idea. And, of course, you can replace the story entirely. I'm not saying that all chapters should start with stories, but storytelling is close to foolproof.

Stories are so attractive that it might be a tempting plan to simply line up all your best stories, tell them one after the next, and declare your book finished. Many autobiographies don't do much more than this.

But for now, aim higher. Don't limit yourself strictly to narrating events. One anecdote after another runs the risk of the deadly "And then I did this ... and then I did that" problem—surface activity but not much substance. Ideally, you would mix in some reflection, some thoughtful digressing, and some attention to extracting larger meanings.

WHAT IS THE MEANING OF "MEANING"?

What do I mean by meaning? It's an important question. I think the answer is a matter of individual taste and judgment. Meanings come in all shapes, sizes, and descriptions, and the nature of meaning could probably be discussed ad infinitum.

In the meantime, I suggest an uncomplicated definition tailored to the needs of your autobiography: *Meaning is the reason something is worth remembering*.

Getting at meanings need not require heavy-duty introspection or philosophizing. In the best stories, meanings emerge on their own and become self-evident. The writer sets the action moving, selects and highlights the telling details, and then steps into the background as the story takes over. The reader grasps the meaning intuitively. If you read some short story masterpieces, you'll see how brilliantly yet plainly this can be done.

Ideally, the meaning of your stories *shows* or is *felt* and doesn't need to be spelled out, and your best stories will do this naturally. But now and then you'll worry that important points are not clear enough and should be made more explicit. To some degree, this goes against the grain of sophisticated writing doctrine: Good writers consider it a failure if meanings have to be explained outright ("The theme of this story is ...") or if readers have to be directly instructed in what's going on. You see this in cartoons or comic books—it's called "signposting" and has the subtlety of a jackhammer.

However, I hope the literary establishment will forgive me, but I think autobiography writers should respectfully disregard subtlety if it creates any risk of obscurity. The goal of your autobiography is not to win a writing contest, and your readers may not be accustomed to literary subtlety. Your purpose is to say certain things to your readers, and if they miss the point, it's *your* fault. So if making meanings clear requires writing key words on your forehead with a marking pen, that's what you should do. If you feel you have to add a sentence beginning "What this story means to me is ...," don't hesitate to do it. Purpose trumps all other motivations.

SELECTION

When you first think about your best stories, only the obvious few come to mind, but once you start stirring around in memory, they'll come back at you in tidal waves. Most writers of autobiographies and memoirs say the hardest part is dealing with the endless supply of stories and other good material, which of course forces difficult decisions on what to put into the book and what to leave out.

In chapter one, I assured you that memory would yield a long list of stories you might want to tell, and you would train yourself to recognize the best stories for your book. This brings us to the important matter of selection.

It is obvious that you will *exclude* more stories than you *include* (unless you want a five-thousand-page final document), but what criteria will you use? Why is one story chosen while dozens of good stories are put aside?

There is no rule book on this. It's up to you. Certain milestone and turning-point stories will obviously get into your book. Other decisions will be dictated by your structure or thematic approach.

Trial and error might be a guide—some stories tell themselves easily and others don't. And sometimes particular stories jump out of your brain and demand inclusion; you just *have* to tell them.

As you spend time writing your stories it will become clear which ones provide the most value and demand selection. The best stories allow you to describe or make sense out of things or reveal meanings or pin down memories. They help you learn (and teach) lessons about behavior or the nature of life. You might *start* many different stories but the ones you'll *keep* are the ones that do these things.

A Highly Admired Talent

My family was blessed with one storyteller who became something of a legend. He was my paternal grandfather, called "The Doc" (he was a dentist). At every family gathering, there would come a moment when everyone would assemble in the living room (the modern equivalent of huddling around the campfire). The adults would hush the kids, and The Doc would hold forth, recounting favorite yarns from days gone by.

Everyone listened avidly even though the stories had been heard many times before. People waited for punch lines and roared with laughter. They welled up with emotion. They winked and sighed and clapped. They sat back beaming with pride and pleasure. They made sure the children got the points and absorbed the lessons.

The Doc *was* good. He had a way of reaching everybody and he knew when to stop. Afterwards we would say to each other, "That man can really tell a story." It was a highly admired talent. It always has been.

I suspect that stories have a greater lifespan than other forms of information, probably because they weave information into experience. Stories seem to plant themselves in permanent memory. You pass a TV and catch a glimpse of a movie

YOU DON'T HAVE TO BE FAMOUS

you haven't seen in three decades, but you remember it. Or someone starts telling a joke, and you stop them—you heard that story in eighth grade.

You can tell a lot of facts, and people will forget them immediately. Build them into a story, and they might be remembered forever. So an answer to "How do I achieve posterity?" is "Tell stories."

FRAGMENTS

Some of the memories that come back to you as you write your autobiography are not stories; they're only fragments of stories.

But some fragments, like a broken toy in the attic, can illuminate a memory with a candlepower far beyond what you expected. Don't exclude them because they don't seem to qualify as full-fledged stories.

Let me give an example of a memory fragment.

There was a man named Al, now dead, a relative by marriage on my father's side. He and my father were about the same age. They were friends growing up.

Al was a self-made man and a dominating alpha male. He was brawny, six-foot-six, boisterous, and somewhat raw—a hard-to-miss, cigar-chomping character.

I saw little of him growing up and probably never said more to him than hello and good-bye until a conversation that took place when he was beginning to fade, and I was in my mid-fifties. We found ourselves at a family gathering in Chicago, briefly sharing the same table at a sidewalk cafe.

He didn't recognize me, but when I introduced myself, his face lit up, and he immediately related a memory of my (long-deceased) father. Al's words went something like this: "I remember your dad and me; we were at this fancy wedding party at some hotel just before the war [World War II] and went out for a break. It was freeze-your-ass-off cold out there, but we were so full of booze, we didn't feel a thing. Just sat on the steps in our shirt-sleeves and had a smoke and shot the breeze."

That was it. After he told it, he smiled and then shrugged. An emotion flicked across his face, and I could see the memory had a meaning he couldn't articulate. He'd described a moment in which nothing much had happened, but more than a half-century later, it was still vivid in his mind.

In the weeks that followed, I kept thinking about that image of the two young men smoking on the hotel steps. I realized that it was now in *my* mind as vividly and permanently as it was in Al's.

A wedding had taken place in New York City in late 1941, a short time before the attack on Pearl Harbor drew America into world war and changed the lives of my father and Al's generation.

The wedding was followed by a gala party at a splendid Manhattan hotel. At some point beyond midnight, after considerable alcohol and revelry, long after the men had shed their tuxedo jackets, and the women had kicked off their high heels, Al and my father had gone outside together for a cigarette and a shared moment of fresh air.

It was probably a Saturday night. Hotel guests, bundled against the cold, were returning from their nights on the town, emerging from taxis and scurrying past these two men sitting together on the hotel steps.

They were both about thirty, and for both of them, the curtain was going up on an exciting time of life. They were newly married and starting families (my mother was pregnant with me at this time). They faced the prospect of war, a scary but also dramatic future. They sat and smoked and talked for a few minutes before going back inside.

Everything else from that evening is long forgotten, but this snapshot survives. It's just an image, but it captures a significant moment. Al's few rough sentences were an inadvertent gift to me, illuminating a turning point in my father's life.

And it was cinematically perfect. A Hollywood screenwriter could not frame a better scene: The young men sitting in the winter air on the steps of a ritzy hotel with a dance orchestra audible in the background. A director would add softly falling snow. But who knows, maybe it *was* snowing. Maybe softly falling snow drove them back inside.

The mental image I have of that moment is better than a thousand photographs—and in fact I have no photos of my father at that age, so this is the *only* imagery of my father in the years before I was born, when he was in the prime of young manhood. I feel that I can see him and even know him as he was that night, as if I'd sat on those steps myself. That's a lot of value from a tiny fragment of time in which almost nothing happened beyond some forgotten talk and the smoking of a cigarette.

Don't Set a Trap for Tomorrow

Let's say you're writing a great story about the day you got a big raise and then went out and bought your spouse a new car. You remember the day perfectly, and your account of it is emerging with effervescent energy.

But then you glance at the clock and see that your allotted writing time is running out. You could work overtime and complete the story—that's what you *want* to do because its momentum is carrying you along enjoyably—or you could put on the brakes somewhere between the promotion and the car purchase, leaving the rest of the story for tomorrow.

Which should you do?

Good advice would be: Stop and finish tomorrow because tomorrow your eagerness to finish the story will bring you to your desk promptly and eagerly. You'll know exactly what to do and where to begin and you'll throw yourself right into it, getting back into stride without a hitch. You'll have momentum on your side, and with luck, it will carry you beyond the car-buying story and into the next thing.

But if you take the other approach and finish the story today, you'll have two options when you return to your desk tomorrow: Spend your writing session admiring what you wrote yesterday or face the blank-page challenge of breaking the ice on something new.

This is not a problem if you clearly know what to write next. But what's bad to be facing is the "What do I do now?" question without an answer. As I've said, this is always a perilous position, a dead stop in which you're vulnerable to writer's block and other bad influences, such as laziness or discouragement. Writers defeat writer's block with momentum, but you've just spent your momentum in a writing binge you should have restrained. This is especially undesirable when it happens at the gates of something new, a new section or chapter.

Writers are always facing blank pages, but avoid doing this in a no-momentum condition. Getting to the end of a story or chapter should not be a signal to get up and leave your desk. Either leave it unfinished or finish it but blast on to the next thing before quitting for the day, always trying to

YOU DON'T HAVE TO BE FAMOUS

give yourself something to resume tomorrow. You're setting a potential trap for yourself if you finish a writing session without knowing how the next session will begin.

WHAT IS A STORY?

As you evaluate your stories and try to decide which to select for your book, it helps to understand what a story *isn't*. Events are not necessarily stories. Activity is not, in itself, a story. Details and data are not stories. A capsule summary is not much of a story.

What is *really* not a story—but often tries to be one— is a sequence of miscellaneous things that are united only by the fact that they happened. This is a hazard in telling about your life, and for an illustration of how undesirable it is, think back to your last family gathering when Aunt Esther went off on one of her deadly narratives about the old days.

"Then in '72 or '73, I forget which," she said, "we moved up to Grand Rapids and Cliff bought that car from France with the muffler that kept falling off, and it was the summer when Ellen broke her leg at the beach and her cousin—I think his name was Gus— drove all the way from Falmouth, or was it Yarmouth, and had an accident, and we lent him the French car, which he totaled, so that was the end of that. And the next thing was Cliff getting transferred to Milwaukee, and we had that flood in the basement, and I got the fellow from next door, Howard Smith or Jones, to come over in his fishing boots and turn off the water, finally. Do you remember, hon?"

No, Uncle Cliff is on the couch gazing at the football game on TV, tuning out Esther's rambling like everyone else. Aunt Esther is not telling *stories*. What's coming out of her mouth is just random and disjointed yackety-yak. It is relentlessly pointless and because it is pointless, it becomes painful.

In spoken conversation you can sometimes get away with telling nonstories, but the discipline of writing won't tolerate it. Writing forces you to tell a story by the rules, which are simple and obvious. Once you've learned them, you'll easily see the difference between stories and non-stories. This will help you spot nuggets in unsuspected places and dismiss some ideas before you waste time on them. Your sense of what a story is—and isn't—will be a major factor in your book's success.

So what are the rules? Deep thinkers from various writing establishments have propounded intimidating formulations and jargon to answer this question, but I try to keep it simple.

If you ask a teacher to define a story, the traditional answer begins with, "It has to have a beginning, a middle, and an end." Students snicker at this, but later they might realize what a valuable thought this is: A story must have forward movement. It has to go somewhere, and I don't mean from Grand Rapids to Milwaukee. It has to go somewhere in a way that involves something significant happening—something changing.

Change is an indispensable requirement for a story—change in the sense of a transformation that has a meaningful effect on one or all of the people involved in the story. This suggests a life-shaping insight or a large moral lesson, but, of course, we know that good stories exist at even the humblest levels. Big insights and

YOU DON'T HAVE TO BE FAMOUS

moral lessons are not required; sometimes the change can be small and subtle, implicit in a fleeting moment or a feeling, such as a few minutes on some hotel steps on a cold night long ago.

In this vein, I think of the late columnist Erma Bombeck, who told endlessly delightful stories about the housewife experience. In her hands, a struggle with an uncooperative sponge mop would capture every necessary element of a good story.

Would such stories have a place in autobiography? Absolutely. Would they qualify as significant? Yes, in a modest way. Is significance restricted to major events, the triumphs and tragedies of life? No, no, no, no, no.

So don't be intimidated if your stories lack Shakespearean depth or global magnitude. It is not necessary for a story to include an earthquake that kills forty thousand people or a trauma that causes a person to reject Wall Street and become a missionary in Bhutan.

In fact, I think small, personal experiences often make for far *better* autobiographical material than titanic events (such as Pearl Harbor, the assassination of JFK, 9/11), possibly because we share in a group reaction to big events while the small ones are uniquely our own.

Earlier, I mentioned an incident in my family that caused a three-year break between an aunt and uncle. The event itself was minuscule—a single spoken sentence in which the *words* were acceptable but a *tone of voice* caused a deep stab of hurt feelings. The wound was painful and lasting. Fortunately, the brother and sister later reconciled, but imagine the situation if one had died, and the other had to live on with the memory of a central life relationship poisoned by a tone of voice? *That* would be a story.

The significance of the change that takes place in a story might take many forms, but it's obvious that the change that resonates with the greatest meaning is emotional. Remember my simple definition of meaning: *the reason something is worth remembering*. You have a strong memory of something that happened fifty years ago, and you *feel* something when you remember it—that's strong proof that it had meaning.

Another critical ingredient of a story, sometimes overlooked, is the need to be *interesting*. Earlier, I mentioned the need to be entertaining, and in my view *entertaining* and *interesting* are about the same thing, although *entertaining* might imply frivolous crowd-pleasing while *interesting* is more serious.

The dazzling Tom Wolfe prefers the e-word and proposes a writing commandment illustrating its priority, "First, entertain." But whichever word you prefer, the challenge of storytelling requires capturing and holding the reader's attention.

This in turn requires two realizations that do not come easily to the Aunt Esthers of the world.

First, you must accept that your stories are not interesting to others simply because they happened.

Second, you must accept that others may not automatically grasp the interest value or significance of your story even when *you* feel it palpably. It is your job as the storyteller to extract it, to reveal the value of the story and make readers feel it too.

Listen to Aunt Esther's gab about moving to Milwaukee and Ellen's broken leg and Gus totaling the French car and Mr. Smith or Jones stopping the flood in the basement— this is classic "And then I did this ... and then I did that"

YOU DON'T HAVE TO BE FAMOUS

jabbering, and its meaninglessness drives you crazy. But a good writer like Erma Bombeck might have looked just a little deeper into each of these *events* and turned them into memorable *stories*—with beginnings, middles, and ends, with meaningful transformation and interesting change.

How does a writer make a story interesting? Or, even more difficult, how does a writer make a subject interesting to a reader who is *not* interested?

Start with the premise that if there's something you want to write about, there's something about it that is interesting *to you*. So the trick is to identify this element and communicate it effectively to readers.

When Ernest Hemingway was teaching himself to write, he would spend hours in art museums staring at great paintings, trying to pick out the specific details that gave a painting its power. He believed that if he mastered the skill of pinpointing the elements that created meaning in a scene or story, he would then be able to capture them in his writing.

So if you want to tell a story about gardening, hockey, knitting or trading options in pork bellies but sense that your readers might not be automatically fascinated, you have to say, "What is it about this topic or story that makes it universal and would hold anyone's interest?" (If you can't find an answer to this question, you won't be able to write the story.)

In college, I had a great writing teacher, Nancy Huddleston Packer, who would occasionally scrawl in the margin of your short story, "What's at stake here?"

At first I was puzzled by that question, but I now see its importance: Why should the reader *care* about the outcome of this story unless something is at stake? If it's not important to a character in the story, it's certainly not important to the reader. What is going to be gained or lost or felt or learned? The writer has to know what's important about a story and make the reader feel it.

A good truck driver can drive his truck down a mountain without once stepping on the brakes, controlling his speed by downshifting into the right sequence of eighteen gears. Why should I care? I have never driven an eighteen-gear vehicle and barely understand what this means, and I'm confident I'll never need to do it myself.

But, as John McPhee explains in his book *Uncommon Carriers*, how about if what's at stake for the driver is an affirmation of his skill and the pride he takes in it, and the way it enriches his life. *That* is why it's important to him, and it's something I can understand and admire. Understanding it, I can now read a story about truck driving that I previously would not have cared about for a millisecond.

It would be good preparation for writing your autobiography to read some of today's superlative nonfiction writers like McPhee or Bill Bryson, who have the gift of taking topics you thought you could never care about and turning them into great storytelling. Study how they do it, how they find the story elements that would interest any reader.

It is not beyond you to do the same. If you love gardening, it is worth a major effort to articulate *why* gardening appeals to you. Once you've done that, your readers will see it through your eyes. Your book will be much enriched. And you might be enriched too, with a better understanding of something you never really thought about.

This is good news for unfamous autobiographers because it levels the playing field with the Winston Churchills of the world. Your stories may not be as momentous as theirs, but they can be just as good, maybe better, if you put your heart into telling them well.

YOU DON'T HAVE TO BE FAMOUS

11

WRITING ADVICE FOR THE LONG HAUL

I've said several times that most of the problems that seriously threaten your writing effort will be encountered early. The upside is that when you've put those hazards behind you, you'll have good grounds for optimism that you're going to make it all the way. If you've come this far reading *this* book, that's a good sign that you're a finisher.

Once you've written a chapter, you'll know what it is to write a chapter of autobiography. That's a big step in the learning process, and you'll find that improvements and a greater comfort level will follow quickly.

The aim of this chapter is to provide general advice that will be useful as you settle into the long haul of writing your book.

SHOWING VERSUS TELLING

"Painting a word picture" is a cliché, but it's a good one: Using words that *show* what happened is often better than *telling* it.

Here's *telling*: "Ginny was elated when she won the tournament. It was very emotional."

Compare that with *showing*: "When Ginny won the tournament by sinking that three-foot putt, a roar went up from the crowd, and she hurled her putter into the air and dropped to her knees, covering her eyes because she couldn't stop sobbing."

Showing makes the reader an eyewitness to the scene. You *see* Ginny sinking the putt, hurling her putter, dropping to her knees sobbing, and you hear the crowd roar. Knowing that it was a three-foot putt makes the picture even sharper.

Showing usually describes action better than telling. And when a scene's meaning or emotion is implicit in the action, showing it well might make telling superfluous.

And showing is not limited to obvious physical signals such as hurling a putter. If you wanted to *tell* how supportive Ginny's parents were, you could back it up with imagery showing Mom getting up early every day to drive Ginny to golf lessons and Dad working extra shifts to pay for those lessons.

Of course meanings and emotions are not always expressed in physical action, and it's a mistake to rely solely on outward detail. Showing has its limits and there are countless examples of good writers showing almost no details. The force of their narratives carries the weight and they don't bother describing the weather or the room or tones of voice or facial expressions. So it's a mistake to think that everything has to be shown in word pictures or that showing is superior to telling. Both are useful and you should mix them for maximum complementary affect. Show what you can't tell, tell what you can't show, and sometimes do both.

YOU DON'T HAVE TO BE FAMOUS

The weakest tools for descriptive writing are adjectives and adverbs. You will find them all over your first draft but as you examine them individually, you'll be surprised at how little they contribute. If you've shown Ginny hurling her putter and falling to her knees sobbing, you hardly need to point out that she was *elated* or *emotional*. Try to eliminate every adjective that doesn't add significant clarity or meaning—a noun is much better off alone than with a predictable or inadequate modifier.

BE SPECIFIC

Specific details create sharper focus as the reader visualizes a scene. "It snowed twenty-five inches, so with each step, I was stepping into snow above my knees" is superior to "It was a really big snowstorm."

Specificity also enhances the strength and substance of your stories. "Barbara was class president with a 3.9 grade point average and was confident of getting into Duke, but I was secretly nervous for her because I'd read that Duke rejected more than 80 percent of its applicants." "The day I bought my house, August 2, 1990, was the biggest financial down day of my life—in the same ten minutes in which I signed a huge check for the house, someone rushed into the lawyer's office and told us that Iraq had invaded Kuwait, causing a stock market crash that sent the rest of my estate through the floor."

What do you think of this: "The flight to Brazil was the most incredible flight of my life."? The flaw is that the writer is assuming the reader will correctly understand the intended meaning of *incredible*, which could be good (anticipation of the fun you'd have in Brazil) or bad (a terrifying storm shook the plane) or extremely annoying (because of lost luggage, a long delay, and disgusting airliner food). I don't object to the colloquial adjective *incredible*—it probably fits the writer's voice—but it's necessary to follow up quickly with clarifying specifics.

In the same spirit, you sometimes need to attach specific or literal language to interpret figurative language, making sure the reader gets the point. If you write, "Dan didn't go to work just to eat his lunch," your reader might be mystified, but if you write, "Dan was a smart, active, contributing guy—he didn't go to work just to eat his lunch," then you've spelled out your point and underscored it with colorful language.

A specific detail, when it's a *perfect* detail, sometimes makes a deeper and more memorable impression than everything else in a story, but you have to be discriminating because specificity can backfire when it introduces detail that is insignificant or distracting. "Pat bought a Kazuko A800 with 6X optical zoom and 6.0 pixels" is good if the specifications of the camera are relevant to the story, but it's overkill if the point is simply that "Pat bought a new camera."

Being highly specific about a particular detail is often a writer's way of signaling the reader that the detail will become important later in the story. If you write, "Todd came over around midnight carrying a chainsaw," you should realize that the chainsaw is a signal of imminent menace or mayhem, and you'd better deal with it. If Todd only wanted to talk sports or borrow a cup of sugar, the presence of the chainsaw is a false signal that unbalances the whole story. You're better off not being specific about the chainsaw.

A final point about specificity: Use names. It's a rule of all local newspapers to get as many names as possible

YOU DON'T HAVE TO BE FAMOUS

into the paper, simply because people like to see their names in print. It's a good idea for your book for the same reason and also because you never know who will read it or what questions they'll have. Think of names as specific details that focus memory—saying, "Phil came to dinner and brought a date" is not as good as "Phil came to dinner and brought a date, Jenny Wilson from San Diego."

I've read an amateur autobiography in which the writer happily declares that his son made three lifelong friends in his first week at college. But he doesn't give their names. I was one of the three friends (and would have been delighted to see my name in his book), and I know who the second friend is, but neither the son nor I can guess the identity of the third friend. It's a tantalizing question, but the writer has died, and we'll never know the identity of the person who did *not* turn out to be a lifelong friend.

CHANGE PACE

Over the long haul of a book, it's refreshing to vary the energy level as well as the mood and tone. Stories or emotions peak, but then the narrative subsides for a while as you move into something new. This is good. Readers recognize and welcome changes of pace.

Sometimes ebbs and flows are instinctive, other times they're intentional. If a chapter ends with something emotionally powerful, it might be good to give the reader a break by starting the next chapter with something light. If a chapter is packed with action (a strong, front-door opening; lots of events; short, punchy sentences; active verbs; lots of *showing*), start the next chapter by gearing down and being more reflective (an introspective, side-door start, lots of *telling* using thoughtful language and evocative detail).

Sometimes the writer's voice and presence should be assertive—for instance, when commenting on a scene or digressing (in a way that turns out to be relevant)—but at other times, the writer should slip into the background and let the narrative take over. Follow serious with humorous. Switch from ordinary events to life-changing events.

No matter how good your book is, sameness is wearying, so try to insert a few surprises—not staggering jolts or violent transitions but some unexpected moves or angles that show readers you're not in a rut.

Humor: High Risk, High Reward

Humor is indispensable in your autobiography. Humor is everywhere, and, as we all know, many things that were far from funny when they happened are hilarious in retrospect. And retrospect is what autobiography is all about.

You should be sure to include the funny stories of your life, but you will also discover that some of the best comedy arises spontaneously as you write. You'll be telling a story, and there it is, something you might never have seen or suspected. It just comes out—if you let it. The key is to have confidence in it and resist a temptation to ignore it because it seems frivolous or unworthy.

Years ago, I had a conversation with the great humorist Calvin Trillin, who has published numerous funny books and many funny stories in *The New Yorker*. I complained to him that I had submitted a number of humor pieces to the magazine, but all were rejected even though I was convinced that at least a few of them were genuinely funny.

YOU DON'T HAVE TO BE FAMOUS

"*Too* funny, probably," he said.

That stopped me. "Too funny? They rejected humor pieces because they were too humorous?"

"That's right," he said. "I've had a lot of those rejections."

There is always a right *level* of humor. The humor level on a nightclub stage in Las Vegas is very different from the level appropriate to a business meeting or a conversation in a crowded elevator. *The New Yorker's* goal in those days—it's clearly different now—was a chortle of sophisticated appreciation for the author's charming wit. *Not* a laugh-out-loud guffaw, which was probably what I was seeking, being *too* funny.

In your autobiography, you should develop a sense of the right level of humor and be consistent. If you're a naturally funny person, this might require some restraint; if you're not normally funny, it might require giving yourself some permission to loosen up.

Risk-taking is inherent in humor and failure creates a resounding thud. Comedians call it "bombing" and say, "I *died* out there." (They also describe triumphant success in death imagery: "I *killed* out there," and death figures in a famous punch line about being professionally funny: "Dying is easy. Comedy is hard.") I think being funny in print is generally harder and riskier than being funny face-to-face. Earlier, I mentioned sarcasm as an especially dangerous thing in print because some readers will miss its sarcastic intent. You have to decide for yourself whether amusing many of your readers is worth leaving a few of them baffled.

Here's some gentle advice about being funny in your book: Underdoing is better than overdoing. Have fun, but keep in mind that a little goes a long way. It's amazing how little humor is required to create a feeling that you are a delightful writer even though you never tried to leave readers in stitches.

Here's some strong advice about being funny in your book: Don't let trying to be funny reveal underlying malice. (Stephen King says, "Humor is anger with its makeup on.") Humor is frequently at someone's expense and can be very cruel. What might be good-natured teasing or acceptable ribbing in a social situation can be brutal in print, leaving a lifelong wound. There's a big difference between saying the unsaid (which can be hilarious) and saying the unsayable (which can be an atrocious breach of taste or judgment). If instinct suggests you're approaching the unsayable, back off.

Another caution involves vulgarity, even on a seemingly harmless kindergarten level. Vulgarity has produced a high percentage of the laughs in human history, but it misfires on the printed page, especially if you're writing for posterity (future generations might be appalled by your giggly account of Joan's somewhat inebriated antics at that party). The impact of vulgarity is just too much, too rude. It's a cheap laugh; writing it might be tempting, but you'll wish you hadn't.

Finally, here's my strongest advice about being funny in your book, and if you ignore it you'll be sorry: Never try to be funny about anything involving race, religion, ethnicity, disease, and death, and be very careful about sex. No matter how innocent you are, and even if the joke is partly on you, going into these areas in print invites ugly consequences, marks you as a fool, and will probably discredit your whole book.

Two small tips about rewriting humor writing: One, if you write something spontaneously, and it's funny, don't tinker with it. Humor is delicate, and tinkering is likely to destroy the subtle magic that caused the laugh. Two, apply the Wince Test. Come back the next day and re-read your funny section out loud. If you wince, kill it.

"EXPLAINITIS" AND THE ROLE OF INSTINCT

Most people visiting their dentists dread the pain, but I dread the monologue. My dentist does a fine job with my teeth, but the man never stops gabbing. He actually uses the introductory phrase, "To make a long story long," and then he does just that.

Every story goes on until you want to scream, which of course would not surprise a dentist unless he realized the true cause. And I know that dentists are in an odd situation, having to conduct one-sided conversations because the patient's mouth is full of fingers and dental tools that prevent any response beyond primitive grunts.

What you realize when someone is boring you senseless is that it makes you feel angry, possibly because you feel trapped. It is like being forced to listen to a comedian who isn't funny—you just can't stand it.

E.B. White said, "It is seldom advisable to tell all," but once we get rolling there's a tendency to tell all and then some. This is known as "overtelling" or "explainitis."

A red warning light should go on to alert the writer to an explainitis situation. Let's hope the writer sees the light *before* the reader and conducts emergency surgery, removing repetition, condensing, chopping anything unnecessary, maybe deleting the whole section.

But how do you know you've rattled on too long? The rewriting process will help—after you've been over a certain passage many times it will become very clear if it's too long. But even more important is instinct. Very important writing advice is: *Always listen to your instincts*. And not just about overtelling.

It happens sometimes that you suddenly just know that something's not working, as if a buzzer had gone off. You don't know what or why, and, in fact, your impulse is to defend and preserve what you've written. But I've learned that from the moment instinct sends you the slightest hint of a signal—a sentence is clunky, a direction is wrong, something you're saying doesn't seem to make sense—the verdict is in. It's decided, and the only question is how long you'll resist until you kill it or fix it.

Sometimes a simple cut will solve the problem, but often a laborious repair job is called for. The lazy side of you would prefer to skip it for now and hope the problem goes away before instinct sends you a second warning. But don't wait, it's a bad habit. Now is better.

In autobiography, the incentive to cut or fix anything that risks boring the reader should be tremendous: Do you want to risk having people yawning or looking at the clock just as you're telling the most important stories of your life?

WHAT TO DO WHEN YOU BOG DOWN

In chapter seven, I made four suggestions about responses to writer's block: take a break, delete all writing contaminated by writer's block, write only in short sentences, and find *something* you can write, anything that gets you moving.

These suggestions are also useful when you bog down, not necessarily because of writer's block. Now let me add five new suggestions.

1. When in doubt, leave it out. Probably no other rule solves problems as often as this one. If rules of writing had batting averages, this one would be close to a perfect 1.000.

If there's a particular point you just can't write—the words won't come or the idea won't focus—just drop it.

YOU DON'T HAVE TO BE FAMOUS

Write around it or just forget about it and skip on to the next thing. The odds say this will improve the chapter instead of hurting it—the *absence* of the difficult passage will never be noticed while its *presence* would be a sore thumb.

Deleting might not be a long-term solution; if you notice something missing when you come back to rewrite, you'll have to make another try at it, but for now, lighten your load and move on.

2. Tell it to your aunt. This is a great tip that I learned in my TV news-writing days. If you're mired in the mud and just can't write the story, put all your bad tries aside and place an imaginary phone call to your aunt (or any friend or relative who is bright but not specifically knowledgeable about the story you're trying to write).

Imagine your aunt's facial expression as she earnestly tries to understand your explanation of the story, which you must do *out loud* while holding the phone.

Somehow, speaking aloud activates your inner editor. Talking to a real person (even if there's no one actually at the end of the line) creates a reality that breaks the logjam in your mind. You instinctively jettison the bad baggage that's weighing you down—the verbal clutter, showing off, excess complexity, or indecision about what you're trying to say.

You might stumble for a while, but it's remarkable how quickly the right language and focus come. But remember, as with the Wince Test, you must speak *out loud*. You might feel silly and self-conscious, but it's worth it.

You might also try *reading* aloud. You'll find that a jumbled or convoluted paragraph is hard to read; your lips and tongue refuse to cooperate. After a few painful tries you'll become aware of where the flaw is, and that should help you fix it.

3. Regain your rhythm with a running start. Back up to a place before the trouble started and charge forward again, pretending the bog-down never happened. Don't try to improve or straighten out the bad stuff—generate fresh stuff and allow creative momentum to carry you through.

All these suggestions involve shaking off the *cramp* that writer's block puts on the natural flow or rhythm of your writing. I've never forgotten a scene from the movie *Butch Cassidy and the Sundance Kid* (1969, written by William Goldman). The Sundance Kid, played by Robert Redford, is trying to prove his identity to a disbelieving codger who demands that Sundance demonstrate his legendary skill as a gunslinger.

The codger, played by Strother Martin, throws an object onto the ground about twenty feet away and orders Sundance to shoot at it. (I've seen this scene a number of times but cannot figure out what the object is—it looks like a tobacco packet.)

Sundance begins his full gunfighting motion, but the codger stops him and says, "No, no, none of that fancy stuff, just point the gun and shoot." Sundance takes two shots but misses badly.

The codger snorts in derision and starts to turn away. Sundance then does his full motion—knees, hips, hands, eyes, crouch, balance, and so on. This time he's dead-on. His bullets hit the object and make it dance in the dust.

Rhythm. To be natural, he needed his whole shooting motion. Isolating a single step in the process made him awkward and ineffective. The same is true in writing.

4. Outline the next few pages. Sometimes the discipline of a simple little outline will help you straighten out your thoughts and line them up for clearer telling. I've said that outlines are a threat to creative spontaneity, but if you're bogged down, you've lost your spontaneity anyway.

Treat yourself like a grade school student dealing with elementary questions. What are my three main points? Which should come first, second, and third? How are the three points connected? Make it simple. If something complicates it, you've probably put your finger on the cause of your trouble. Getting rid of it will get you out of the bog.

5. Be guided by purpose. Sometimes the problem is not about rhythm, voice, words, confidence, or minor confusion. You've arrived at a serious content problem, and you have to resort to something we often try to avoid: applied intellectual discipline, also known as *thinking*.

There is a *conflict* in what's brought you to this point or in where you go next. You have to identify the problem, rethink, and maybe change your plan or find a new one. I have learned that when you are looking for a beacon in the darkness, the answer is always *purpose*. Try to steer toward its light, asking yourself: "Okay, what am I trying to do with this? Where am I trying to go, and why?"

Don't expect the writing gods to give you an immediate straight answer. They will make you work for your reward. But remember that writing is a thinking process. Thinking will get you to a good answer eventually, though it might be rough sledding for a while.

You Owe Yourself a Good Ending

You know the end is coming, and so does the reader. As Chekhov predicted, pressure and self-consciousness you haven't felt since the start of the book now surge back as you approach the final pages or paragraphs. Falseness comes into your voice.

The result might be something facile and clichéd, in the "only time will tell" or "the future remains to be seen" category. Or it might be an abdication, a *stopping* instead of an ending as the writer surrenders under the pressure of finding a worthy thought and dives for the exit with hardly a wave or farewell.

What's at stake here is the last impression you give your readers. You've put a lot into this and don't want to fade out weakly at the finish line. It doesn't have to be fancy, but you owe yourself something better than a cliché or an exhausted collapse.

Most good endings are not thought-out in advance. They emerge in the flow, and you *discover* them as they sit there before your eyes. When this happens, be grateful and don't attempt to embellish it. But if this *isn't* happening, fight the impulse to slap down a quick solution and be done with it.

It's always helpful to take a break and let your subconscious work on it for a while. Or take my suggestion about backing up and getting a running start over the paragraphs that are not ending right—maybe *this time* your rhythm and spontaneity will provide the answer.

Another approach is to think back to your original purpose for writing your autobiography and discuss what you've learned while trying to achieve it. Ask yourself questions like, "What have I discovered by writing this autobiography?" or "What meanings or lessons from my life might be instructive to others?"

Seize the value of retrospection and hindsight. Perhaps there is a philosophical idea that's been at the back of your mind; now is the time to move it forward and see if you can develop it.

In corporate work, it is standard to end with the "takeaway," the message you want readers or listeners to take away and remember when all else is forgotten. Closing with the takeaway makes sense in a speech; it may or may not work in an autobiography simply because you might not

YOU DON'T HAVE TO BE FAMOUS

have a final message you want to leave behind. If you don't have one, don't force one.

An ending need not be profound or poetic or witty or inspiring. Keep in mind that this is only the end of a book, not a death scene, so don't be too dramatic and don't get emotionally sloppy. Be sincere, mildly humorous, if possible, and as gracious as possible. Take a modest bow and say good night.

And be brief. I've noticed with some speech makers that there is a tendency, as the end approaches, to try to prolong their final sweet moments in the spotlight. They are enjoying it and suddenly don't want it to end, so they grasp for something more to say and ramble until they fizzle out. It's an obvious mistake.

Don't be like my dentist, making a long story long. A good ending should be just a little abrupt.

TALKING ABOUT
THINGS WE DON'T
TALK ABOUT

Do you remember the court-martial scene from the 1992 movie *A Few Good Men* in which a Marine colonel (played by Jack Nicholson) is drawn into an angry exchange with the defense lawyer (Tom Cruise) and shouts "You can't handle the truth"?

It became a much repeated line, and I'm about to reuse it to pose an important question about your autobiography: *Can you handle the truth?* Or more accurately, because there's always a limit, *how much* truth can you handle?

How *revelatory* will you be?

Be prepared to discover right away that many of the most meaningful experiences of your life will be the hardest to write, largely because they are so emotionally charged and personal. They are private, sometimes secret, possibly even dark. They might fall into the category of *things we don't talk about*—for instance, grievances and betrayals, bad experiences with drugs or alcohol, violence, immoral or criminal behavior, various types of abuse or illness, unforgivable acts, terrible feuds and fights, and other causes of lasting guilt, fear, shame, or regret.

And since you have not gone through life in a vacuum, these highly sensitive memories will almost always involve *relationships*. You might have had a troubled marriage or a wrenching divorce. You might still carry the scars from old defeats or disgraces, failed ambitions, long-ago snubs, or rejections.

There may be family secrets: an earlier marriage unknown to the children or a long, illicit affair that no one (or everyone) knew about. Perhaps there was an abortion, or a child was given up for adoption.

Whatever your involvement with these deeds—as perpetrator, victim, or innocent bystander—you might have lived many years with the intense emotions they created still boiling inside you.

Sometimes the problem is less about privacy than pain. The experience hurts so much—a death, illness, accident, a disastrous mistake, or misjudgment—that you simply cannot approach it. Perhaps fear of doing so has held you back from writing autobiography.

And here's one more category of things we don't talk about: memories that are wonderful or beautiful but not discussable because they would hurt others—for instance, romantic or sexual experiences, which might be remembered as peak moments in your life. Excluding them from your life story seems wrong, but can you write about them in a book that will be read by your spouse, children, and family?

There is an old saying that nobody gets through life unscathed. Every life story has its misfortunes, mistakes, regrets, and secrets. Every potential autobiographer has a different tolerance for beaming light into this dark chamber.

It's a difficult problem. Now let's make it even more difficult.

Writing about your life is not just about you. It is one thing to make a brave disclosure decision about yourself, but what happens when those disclosures force you to drag other players into the spotlight, to reveal private things about other people? And, of course, disclosure affects not only you *and* the people you write about but *also* your readers, who might be aghast at what you are revealing and affected for the rest of their lives.

The "talking about things we don't talk about" problem starts out as a comfort zone issue but escalates into a moral and ethical issue. We are talking about violating other people's privacy and exposing them to disclosure that might affect them in a profoundly painful way, not only causing emotional distress but even threatening their standing in their families and communities, perhaps even creating scandals that might jeopardize their jobs or well-being.

And these people are not public figures or celebrities who are fair game to writers. On the contrary, they have a right to privacy, and it should not be threatened by you, of all people—a trusted friend or family member.

Keep in mind that while your autobiography might be about posterity for you, you're also creating what might be a highly negative posterity for others by portraying them in some of their worst moments. Even if you've printed only a dozen copies of your book, to them it is like having their secrets broadcast on the evening news.

How would *you* feel about having your privacy violated or being told that your privacy is secondary to someone else's quest to reveal the whole truth and nothing but the truth?

You cannot write autobiography without running into this issue.

MAYBE YOU SEE IT DIFFERENTLY

I've been listing topics and memories that many people would recoil from discussing and would fight to the death to conceal, but perhaps your attitude is just the opposite: You are writing your autobiography because you *want* to discuss and examine them. You want to bring things out, not hold them in.

You regard your autobiography as a kind of self-administered therapy in which you explore and come to terms with the difficult experiences of your life. Your emotions about these events might be so large, you can no longer bear to keep them buried. You want to get things off your chest, make a clean breast, find release or healing. You need to tell your stories openly and freely, without self-censorship, and autobiography is your chosen medium.

This makes sense, and it is a logical impulse to select autobiography for this purpose. One of the first great Western autobiographies was written by St. Augustine (354–430 A.D.), describing his lusting and dissolute ways and subsequent conversion to religious devotion. Its title was *Confessions*.

Confession (always linked to redemption) remained the model for autobiographical writing for more than a thousand years until the Renaissance when entertainment became more popular than redemption. In recent years, confessing seems to have made a popular comeback as writers ranging from students to celebrities seem to have shed an older generation's inhibitions about revealing intimate details in public. This is, after all, a time when you can turn on afternoon television to see people confessing to astonishingly shameless and sordid behavior, usually sexual or violent or both.

Such trashy antics and exhibitionist confessions are not to be confused (I hope) with the efforts of serious people whose motivation and priority is to reflect on the major events and deepest feelings of their lives. It is not surprising if a significant percentage of these writers want to leave behind something more substantial than a cosmetic record of their lives. Or at least they want to process their memories of those occasions through an adult lens, without covering up the blemishes.

The dilemma, of course, is that the subjects they most want to write about are also the subjects that raise the most sensitive disclosure issues. So what we have here are two dramatically different approaches to handling the truth in autobiography. One approach plays it safe and conservative by limiting disclosure, the other is inclined to be boldly revealing and tell all.

I'd like to discuss both, assuming that your likely choice will be something in between. My guess is that you will start with a tilt toward disclosure but, seeing the early results, retreat toward restraint.

I'd also like to say that *either* of these approaches, even though they're polar opposites, can lead you to a valuable writing experience and a book that meets all your needs. The question you'll have to answer is: What *are* your needs?

YOU DON'T HAVE TO BE FAMOUS

THE DEFAULT POSITION: SAFE AND CONSERVATIVE

The idea of writing a private, noncommercial autobiography might not have seemed that attractive when I first mentioned it, but now it's starting to look a lot better.

The "juicy" parts of a life story—implying a titillating reading experience or a revealing glimpse behind the curtain of privacy—are often what sell books, and a publisher is not likely to see the merit of any arguments for omitting exactly what prospective readers want to read. But you are your own publisher. You aren't concerned with selling copies. You have the waiver. You make the rules. If you say something is out, it's out.

I've made the point that omission can be a form of lying, but it is nevertheless defensible in a book written for—and to various degrees *about*—a small, private audience of family and friends. It should also be noted that many autobiographers have no intent to deceive; they are not *consciously* omitting but are only behaving as they always do, practicing the personal reserve and discretion of people who've been taught since childhood that certain things are not discussed. We keep these things to ourselves because they are inappropriate for public discourse and potentially embarrassing to others.

If you intend to be guided by personal reserve and discretion—that is, if you set a ground rule that "juicy" material will *not* be discussed—it seems to me that this is just as acceptable a boundary in a private book as it would be in a face-to-face conversation. I remember, years ago, being impressed by an answer given by Johnny Carson when an interviewer pressured him to disclose his salary—Carson said, in effect, "I was taught growing up in Nebraska that you don't talk about how much money you make, and that's how I feel, and that's all I'm saying." The interviewer was silenced, and Carson won instant respect.

Everyone understands that there are private areas in life. Indeed, steering clear of these areas might be a welcome relief to readers who are very content not to be made to witness uncomfortable scenes or hear agonizing thoughts in a book by their mom or dad or brother or sister.

Also, it's important to note that standing back from detailed disclosure or description of sensitive experiences need *not* detract from their dramatic impact as you tell your life story. You don't have to tell all. The *unsaid* and the *simply said* can be equal or superior in power and eloquence to the *extensively said* or the *fully revealed*. If you handle it delicately, the problem can be effectively solved by acknowledging the painful episode or issue but then saying in effect, "I'm not pretending this didn't happen, but this subject will remain private to me."

The easiest solution to dealing with sensitive or emotional material is to sidestep it entirely, and you have this option. But here's a caveat: A book that continually shrinks from open discussion of the most important experiences of a lifetime is giving up an important dimension. Covering trivial events but evading serious ones might not be a satisfying prescription for the life story you want to write. It also runs the risk of creating a sense of incompleteness among readers who feel they are reading a censored or sanitized work. They might even feel that the writer is *cheating* by withholding material that should have been included.

It seems to me that the middle ground or something close to it is the best possible answer. You can adopt a safe default position and write your autobiography without excluding key events but also without revealing too much or going overboard emotionally.

Your solution has to reflect your personality, but as a general rule, I suggest this: In your first draft—read by no one but yourself—lean toward disclosure; in later drafts, if what you've written makes you uncomfortable, tone it down or delete it.

THE BOLD POSITION: TELLING ALL, GOING DEEP

The same waiver that allows you to swim disciplined and restrained laps on the surface also allows you to attempt spectacular dives from the high board, plunging down into the depths of the heart and soul.

The problem, of course, is that while being brutally honest about yourself might be admirable, being brutally honest about others is just brutal.

It is one thing for fiction writers to borrow from real experience (as they often do), possibly betraying confidences but at least disguising their characters' identities. The fiction writer might be able to rationalize this on the basis of art and truth (or marketability).

But conscience puts a limit on how far an autobiographer can go in subjecting real, identified people to damaging disclosures. Before anything else, the writer should rigorously question his or her own motivation. As I said earlier, if underlying motive is dishonorable, such as getting revenge or inflicting punishment or seeking pity or sympathy or self-justification, this is unattractive, to say the least, and you should hurry away from it.

Another factor is the writer's skill. If you are going to perform on the high wire, you'd better be good. If it's going to be R- or X-rated, you'd better be *very* good. Dealing with complex and powerful emotional situations is a challenge for the most sophisticated writer; less capable writers might prudently decide to back off on the grounds that their skills are not equal to the task.

You should also consider my earlier warning that a writer can never underestimate the ability of a certain (small) percentage of readers to misunderstand or misconstrue *anything*. This misreading or "reading in" might extend to believing the writer has said outrageous things that in actuality are not even remotely suggested (e.g., your mentioning that George was never interested in football is interpreted as a direct statement that George is gay). This is a hazard which cannot be dismissed simply because it's irrational. Whenever you can anticipate such misreadings you should make an extra effort to be clear about what you're saying because a big blow-up among readers is not in your interest, even if you are absolutely innocent.

Something I haven't brought up, though it's worth considering, is the possibility of retaliation by readers who are outraged about what you've written about them. This could come in any number of ways, from a punch in the nose to exclusion from a will to lawsuits or threats of lawsuits. Being sued is an experience you definitely don't want, even though it would probably be difficult to win a libel suit against you (and not worth the considerable expense given that your book is generating no profit from which to pay damages).

My suggestion for writers leaning toward extensive disclosure is the same suggestion I offered to conservative writers coming at this problem with an opposite instinct: Go ahead and do it. Or, let's say, *try* it. Give yourself per-

YOU DON'T HAVE TO BE FAMOUS

mission to write an uninhibited first draft. Say everything you want to say and hold back nothing.

Don't show it to anyone else.

Wait a few weeks and reread it. If alarm bells go off in your mind, delete it (and burn the evidence). But if you're encouraged, keep at it. This is something that will need fine-tuning; you will not dash it off successfully in one try, and it would be extremely foolish to do it in a single binge of emotional catharsis.

This is risky writing but also an excellent challenge to step up to a higher level. It will take a certain amount of courage to proceed in this direction, and strength will also be required to abandon it if it's failing, throwing away your large investment of effort and emotion. But if it goes well, your drafts will become more controlled and moderate with each round of revision, meaning that your original excesses will be tempered, leaving you with something sober and sustainable. I've been taking a cautionary position by stressing the consequences of handling sensitive issues badly, but there is also the possibility that they can be handled very well, an admirable writing achievement that would add considerable depth and value to your book.

Another option is to seek a friend's opinion (a friend is probably more objective than a family member). Choose someone with enough discretion and sophistication to understand the disclosure issue in the context of your potential readers. And, of course, choose someone who has no involvement in the episode you're concerned about.

Create a situation in which you can watch this person read your work, because a facial expression might tell you a lot more than their words. I guarantee this session will be uncomfortable, and it should be. And

when the reaction comes, you should take it seriously—
that is, don't get angry and dismiss it if it's not what
you wanted to hear.

One or two experiences like this will bring you to a
new level of wisdom about the degree to which you can
handle the truth. You might then want to do some soften-
ing and trimming, especially of hurtful minor details. If
you're going to risk upsetting your readers, do it for something *serious*, not something gratuitous or trifling, such as
an ill-chosen, low-value adjective.

Now and then you might be able to avoid trouble by
disguising characters, but make sure you disguise them
so well that there is *zero* possibility of figuring out identities. A bad disguise is worse than no disguise at all—the
person's identity is revealed and so is your incompetence
at concealing it. Also, disguise will be difficult to achieve
given that most of your readers are family or friends who
know everything about your life and will easily figure out
who you mean (or jump to the same wrong conclusion
about who you mean).

Asking Permission

If you have written your scenes but continue to feel guilty or
conflicted about whether to keep or kill them, you may have only
one recourse: showing the potentially wounded person what
you've written and asking permission to use it in your book.

Some autobiographers report doing this with positive results. And asking permission *does* seem like a sensible solution. But it goes against the grain in several ways.

First, when you're asking permission, you're inviting someone else to have a say in your writing process. You are coming
close to giving them a right of final approval, or at least the

YOU DON'T HAVE TO BE FAMOUS

right to request specific edits. That is, you have to compromise your viewpoint and editorial control. No writer likes this, even if it's the right thing to do.

Your dislike of this process is multiplied if you're asking *numerous* people for permissions, as you probably are. You will soon feel that your authorship and ownership have been parceled out in many pieces and that a committee has now taken over the writing of your book.

What you want from all of them is unconditional permission, but that's probably not what you will get. More likely, you will see a range of reactions. Once people realize they're being invited to suggest changes, the suggestions will pour in, most of which you won't like. You worked hard on this, and now it seems that everyone is asking you to delete or alter the very things that, in your view, made the writing right.

A second restraint on asking permission is that in addition to exploiting your loved ones and friends by telling personal stories about them, you might now be adding a second and even more unattractive level of exploitation. That is, you might be manipulating their affection for you. Grandma has always given you everything you want, you can talk your little sister into anything, and as for Uncle Carl, give him a little extra attention and flattery and maybe bring him a beer or two, and you'll get your permission.

Certainly no one wants to thwart your effort or cause you to be angry at them. They don't want you to blame them for obstructing this book project that seems to mean so much to you. So there's a good chance they'll say yes even if they really ought to say no.

And in addition to exploiting their affection, you might be exploiting their very human desire to be part of the story, to see their names in print. It's a cliché that famous people, acquiring a book that might mention them, turn immediately to the index and then whip through the pages in search of their names—seeing their names is their number one concern. This isn't just the egomania of the famous; it's the vanity of everybody.

We all want to be mentioned. This desire makes us exploitable. If it means giving approval to a story that's a little negative and embarrassing, maybe that can be overlooked for now (but resented later) given the desire to preserve a place in the book. It's an old joke about celebrities desperate for a mention in a gossip column saying, "I don't care what you write about me, just spell my name right." Gossip columnists are not expected to observe moral and ethical guidelines, but you are not a gossip columnist. Should you do this to people you care about?

Something you'll discover quickly if you go the permission route is that people have an infinitely surprising range of feelings about what constitutes invasion of their privacy or a breach of their confidence. Some people have enormous tolerance, things just run off their back. Others are stunningly oversensitive and easily wounded, the slightest unflattering detail sending them into depression or rage.

The writer despairs of all this fragile humanity and wishes it could be ignored. How nice it would be to just tell the story and not worry about reactions. Of course, the private autobiographer can do this by writing for no one but him or herself, printing just one copy, and keeping it under lock and key.

But for most people, that's not very satisfying. In the end, you will have to work out your own solutions, either by imposing a general rule or by tailoring a different solution for each case or story. You might decide that asking permission of others is just a way of shifting responsibility; the ultimate permission must come from you.

YOU DON'T HAVE TO BE FAMOUS

SENTIMENT VERSUS SENTIMENTALITY

In many moments of life when we most wish to rise to eloquence, we find that we can speak only in insufferable clichés. Other times our voice dries up and we become speechless. Marcel Marceau, the French mime who, of course, performed without speaking, asked, "Do not the most moving moments of our lives find us without words?"

It's true, but writers are word people. We can't say, "I'm going to leave the next five pages blank to express my inexpressible emotions on this subject." Sentiment is especially desirable in an autobiography. You *should* have emotions as you contemplate your life. Now is the time to express them, and writing should help you express them in a way that is precise and under control.

While sentiment (by which I mean *emotion*) is good, *sentimentality* is bad. It's excessive by definition, self-indulgent and embarrassing, and it makes readers squirm. Worse, it's not truthful. It's been said that sentimentality is a form of lying because it overstates or over-dramatizes the truth (at best) or manipulates it (at worst).

A good writer's tool kit includes some dangerous weapons, including evocative powers that can be used in tawdry or downright ugly ways to exploit readers' emotions. The French author Honoré de Balzac boasted that this was an easy trick—name any emotion, he said, and he could create it in just one page. Truth and sincerity were irrelevant—it was just a matter of the writer's skill in using language and imagery that trigger emotions.

Want to make your reader cry? Just describe a little boy holding his dead puppy in his arms. It won't take more than a sentence or two to moisten the tear ducts. It's that simple, and it can be tempting—especially when your intentions are pure and you simply want to convey a feeling which you feel powerfully yourself—but you should rein yourself in because sentimentality is only an inch from sleaziness.

Knowing this, most responsible writers lean hard in the opposite direction, steering sharply, and even coldly, away from anything that suggests milking emotion. You have probably seen a similar restraint by speakers at funerals. Instead of exploiting their listeners' grief, their eulogies are calm, loving, and even humorous. Such speakers are appreciated and their words are remembered. Other speakers who fall apart and wallow in emotion are painful to everyone, even if their emotions are unquestionably genuine.

Does this mean that strong emotion should be watered down or avoided altogether? No, you can't do that. Emotion is essential to the story of your life. Tenderness, love, pain, joy, regret, even nostalgia all have a place in your book, but you have to be clear-eyed (not teary-eyed) in the vision you present.

You probably agree with me, but something will come over you when you approach that story about your wedding day or your child's graduation or the horrible day when a loved one succumbed to disease. You'll want to invoke the waiver and declare a holiday from self-discipline. But this is precisely *not* the time to do that.

And not just because of the manipulation. Another reason is that mushiness and mawkishness are unsustainable, quickly turning embarrassing and unbearable. Imagine being locked in a room with an Irish tenor singing "Danny Boy" over and over. It won't be long until your sentiment for Danny turns into loathing, and you want to bludgeon the tenor with a blunt instrument.

The right attitude at this point is: Okay, I won't *abuse* the power to evoke emotions, but I do need to *develop* it, right? How does a writer create emotion? The answer is: *honestly*.

First, scrutinize the event or moment or emotion and scrub out all traces of cliché because you do not want a cliché controlling your thinking, and you do not want the impact of the story to be diluted by a stale idea. A cliché is just an off-the-shelf standard viewpoint. You can do better.

Second, eliminate unnecessary details and find the just-right details. These right details might be concrete or abstract, large or small. Think hard about this. Think about your wedding day and try to drill through layer after layer of feeling and detail until you find what it was that really shaped the emotion of the event. If it's not the clichéd, wedding-album feeling you were searching for, understand that this is a plus, not a minus.

I was married in the small chapel of a great cathedral, St. Patrick's, in New York City. How this happened, given that I am not Catholic, is a long story, which I'll spare you. The ceremony itself is a blur except for two things. One is that the priest not only got my name wrong (you are not too surprised by this when your name begins with the letter *z*), but he also butchered my wife's name, which was odd given that she had an easy name, and he knew her. I remember joking about whether wedding vows were legally binding if both parties were incorrectly identified.

The second thing is that as I was walking out, married for less than a minute, a stranger approached me, a middle-aged man who put his hand on my shoulder and told me that he had been married for many years, but his wife had recently died. He said he would pray for me to have as good a marriage as he did. He offered his hand, we shook, and then he turned away and was gone.

Everything else about the wedding was planned, staged, social, and, of course, it was a pleasant cliché. This man, however, penetrated the cliché. It took a few seconds until the reaction hit, but I realized that I was married, life had changed, and I was surrounded by good will and high hopes.

If I were writing about my wedding in an autobiography, I would emphasize the two cliché-busters because they were part of the fun but also the seriousness of the day. Of course, I would try to report other details, seemingly more central (such as a surprise drop-in appearance by the mayor of New York, Ed Koch—my wife worked in his administration), but the truth is that I don't recall a thing about the vows I took or the nice speech my sister-in-law gave, and I only vaguely remember who attended. I would not pretend that these elements had any major emotional impact.

Third, it's important to have an idea of the emotional potential of a scene you are about to write, so you can be realistic about your ambition in writing it. Ask yourself: Can this scene be the "10" I want it to be, or, to be honest, is it only a "6"? The answer will instruct you in how to tell it—an honest 6 is better than a hyped and dishonest 10.

Emotion and Principle #16

Principle #16 from *The Elements of Style*—"Use definite, specific, concrete language"—is most valuably applied when you're least likely to think of it, such as when you've become tongue-tied and incapable of translating thoughts into words.

This, of course, describes many emotional situations, and that should be your signal to reach for Principle #16, which will keep you grounded when your emotions seem to call for the *opposite* of Principle #16, something *transcending* the mundane limits of the "definite, specific, and concrete."

But transcendancy is dangerous territory for most of us. We fall on our faces trying to get there. Even the greatest writers know their limits in this regard. In a famous passage in *Madame Bovary*, Flaubert wrote, "Language is like a cracked kettle on which we beat out tunes for bears to dance to, while all the time we long to move the stars to pity." So be warned that when you try to move the stars to pity, the more likely result will be clunky dance music for big animals.

If you would like to see Principle #16 practiced by a master, read Joan Didion's *The Year of Magical Thinking*, a memoir of the year of her husband's sudden death and the fatal illness of her only child, an adult daughter. Didion maintains clinical detachment with tenacious discipline, never breaking down or appealing for sympathy even as she relates the intimate and anguished details of her grieving in terms and language that demonstrate the power of being definite, specific, and concrete.

It is a remarkable writing performance and a lesson in how a writer can keep control and create extraordinary emotional impact *without* surrendering to emotions. Interestingly, she later told an interviewer that writing the book had been easy, "like sitting down and crying."

REWRITING

Elmore Leonard, who knows what he's doing after writing about forty-two mystery novels and thrillers and many of the movies made from them, appeared at a book promotion event I attended in New York City. He was briefly interviewed by a moderator and then took questions from the audience.

One of the first questions came from a man who stood up and delivered a fawning tribute to Leonard's writing style, saying it was so fluid and effortless that it could only be pure genius. Leonard, a gruff Midwesterner who puts on no author's airs, shifted around uncomfortably as the flattery continued, seemingly ad infinitum. Finally, the man seemed to realize the format required him to end with a question, so he asked, "I'm just wondering, do you ever have to do much rewriting?"

Leonard's glare indicated unmistakably that he regarded this as a boneheaded question of the first magnitude. It would become clear that Leonard had nothing but contempt for the image of a first-draft genius; he considered himself a hardworking, meat-and-potatoes craftsman. You could just hear him thinking: *Do I do much rewriting? What do you think writers do all day, boy?*

What he finally said was: "Writing *is* rewriting."

That covered it. Writing *is* rewriting, and if you don't know that, you don't know anything about writing. Leonard was not going to dignify the question with anything more than that. The moderator took a question from elsewhere in the room.

So now I get to pass Elmore Leonard's message along to you: Writing *is* rewriting.

Those great sentences, scenes, characters, plots, and structures do not arrive on a silver platter. True, flights of inspiration and visits to the magic zone provide some rich material and occasional breakthroughs, and it helps to be trained and talented. But it is rewriting that makes writing good: revisiting, reviewing, revising, rethinking, reworking. Craft, long hours, and elbow grease.

As for that fluid and effortless Elmore Leonard style, that's explained by one of his own rules of writing: "If it sounds like writing, I rewrite it."

LEARN TO READ YOUR OWN WRITING

Reading your own work objectively is an acquired skill. You have to learn to overcome your natural inclination to adore everything you've written.

So let's say you've finished writing your draft, and now you're going to read it. You know it's not Shakespeare, but you did your best, and you're experiencing pride of authorship, the literary equivalent of parental pride. You've given life to this baby, nursed it through infancy and countless growth pains, and your instinct is to protect it from critical attacks, even if the attacks come from you.

Another cause of trouble, more sophisticated, is your confident assumption that because you know (or think you know) what you *meant* to say that you've successfully said it.

You *will* it to be there in your words. Not only that, you *will* it to be clear, impressive, compelling, perhaps moving, never boring, and written with a certain special flair, if you say so yourself. It is there in your imagination and your hopes.

But it's not there.

Let's remember the E.B. White quotation I cited earlier: "When you say something, make sure you have said it. The chances of your having said it are only fair." This thought is the underlying premise of rewriting. It should loom over you as a paranoid presence as you rewrite.

You have to learn to see *only what's there*, to see it the same way readers will see it. You have to be deaf to all your inner pleas and protests on behalf of what you've written. You have to master detachment and a willingness to criticize freely and clinically. Every writer needs an editor but *the editor you need first and foremost is you.*

But it's not the *same* you who did the writing. The editor self represents the other side of your brain, the rigorous, rational, questioning, nit-picking, flaw-finding, not-so-easily-pleased side.

You cannot be a good writer without being a good self-editor. Many inexperienced writers simply don't understand that the editing and rewriting that follows the first rough draft is what makes the difference in the quality of their work. They cannot approach the level of quality they're hoping for until this realization sinks in.

YOU DON'T HAVE TO BE FAMOUS

In your self-editing role, you should come to the task with no bias pro or con, no complicating emotion, and no personal stake. You should be able to evaluate what's there and sense what's missing. You can easily admire what's good, and your radar detects things that are not quite right. Your job is to react as you read, and to suggest solutions to your writing self.

Your two selves—writer and editor—will then read through the draft and collaboratively judge *every single thing* as a candidate for change, deletion, or improvement. I'll repeat that: *every single thing*.

Putting your draft aside for a while and coming back to it fresh is something I recommend for almost every aspect of the writing process, but a good break is especially advisable in the transition period between writing and rewriting for this reason: It turns you into an outsider. You look at your work and it's as if you're reading something *written by someone else*. This is exactly what you want—your slate is clean, and you can reread with relative freshness and objectivity.

This valuable detachment won't last long, so make the most of it. It's smart to do a first, quick read, getting a general impression. Lots of things will leap out at you, and you'll want to stop and wrestle with them right away, but don't. Keep reading and preserve your freshness. Think big before you get involved with small changes.

As you go along, you'll have the occasional feeling that the draft is sending you signals. These are valuable instinctive reactions. You might not know exactly what they're telling you—you'll have to decode them later. For now, just underline or highlight or leave a note in the margin and move on.

You'll spot many things you like, but mainly you'll see that there are a lot of gaps, weak spots, breakdowns in prose or logic and other flaws that need fixing or improving. Don't be discouraged if you see problems with everything—if you *don't* see problems with everything, you probably haven't looked hard enough yet. Understand that *all* first drafts need work, often huge work. Your second and third drafts will need work too. This can go on for a long, long time. The surprise is that you'll get to like it.

Get it out of your mind that rewriting is the endgame. It's much more than that. It entails a lot more than what I call pencil editing—small fixes here and there. You have to go through the whole draft many times, making large and small changes that raise the level of the entire work and sometimes transform it dramatically. The better you get at this, the more you find layer after layer of things that can be changed for the better.

You now begin to see your draft in a new light: *The role of the first draft is to give you something to rewrite.*

Most veteran writers relish the start of rewriting because they have left the uncharted territory of Blank Page Kingdom where getting lost and failing completely is an ever-present possibility. Arriving at the *getting-it-right* phase usually means they've reached solid ground. What's ahead is a craftsman's labor, safer and smaller in its demands, more amenable to logic and skill, less dependent on fickle and mysterious creativity.

You now have thousands of words to work with, and you can do this work to your heart's content. As Toni Morrison says, "The best part of it all, the absolutely most delicious part, is finishing it, and then doing it over.

That's the thrill of a lifetime for me: If I can just get done with that first phase, and then have infinite time to fix it and change it."

THE JOY OF DELETING

This is where *less is more* meets *when in doubt, take it out.* These two sturdy pillars of writing wisdom combine in the rewriting process and work wonders together. Once you overcome your defensiveness about deleting, it becomes exhilarating, like a successful diet. Shedding flab provides instant gratification. Everywhere you look, you see candidates for extinction.

So hunt down all your clutter and explainitis and repetition. Slash it away. Search for dull stretches and energy dips. Cut them out. Find ways to leap from the middle of page 7 to the top of page 11 and get rid of everything in between—a bonanza of deletions. Does your nineteen-page chapter feel a little long? Tell yourself you're not getting up until it's down to sixteen pages. You can do it, and it will be an improvement nine times out of ten.

Believe me when I tell you, there will be plenty of deletable material in your first draft, and the best favor you can do for the draft is to grab the shears and start pruning.

Never get into the high-school mentality of measuring quality by length or being reluctant to cut because you're worried your chapter will be too short. As you eliminate weak material, you'll expose strong material, and since strong material tends to generate *more* strong material, you'll make up for all the weak pages you've deleted and length won't be a problem. But if you do run short, remember that short is usually better than long.

THE MORE YOU LOOK, THE MORE YOU FIND

Years ago, I read an article about how writers feel about critics—always a fun subject because the writers get to lash back and always do so colorfully (for example, John Osborne's "Asking a working writer what he thinks about critics is like asking a lamppost what it feels about dogs.")

What stuck in my mind was Norman Mailer's answer to a question about how he felt about critics sniping at his prose. I'll paraphrase his response: Look, I've been over each page fifty times, maybe one hundred times. I've challenged every word and asked every question. I've been more critical than any critic. I've made endless changes to get it right. No reader could know this work as well as I do. So now a critic comes along and speed-reads it once, probably under deadline pressure, and pronounces judgment. How can I take that opinion seriously?

Well, let's briefly stick up for the critic: A fresh view might see things that are blind spots to the author. But my point is that Mailer, like other writers, has been through his pages many times, scrutinizing *everything*.

I think the process compares to those old "What's Wrong With This Picture?" puzzles. At first glance, nothing seems wrong. But as you study it, defects start appearing everywhere. The same thing will happen with your prose.

Sometimes you read a paragraph a dozen times before noticing a mistake that should have been flagrantly obvious from the start. And you think: *Thank God I found this before anyone else saw it.* This makes you even more compulsive about searching for other mistakes.

Rewriting is a humbling experience. It starts out as a simple process of trial and error, but you're quickly shocked at the number of trials you're conducting to deal with more errors than you ever suspected. But the good news is that the fixes and improvements you're making are convincing evidence of progress. Your work is getting better, maybe much better, and it's not an illusion.

One Hundred Things to Fix

I've said that you should challenge *everything* when rewriting, looking for *anything* that might need correcting or improving. But what do I mean by *everything* and *anything*?

I wanted to see if I could come up with one hundred things that might need work as you go through your draft. It was easy. Think of the list below as a sampling of criticisms and raised questions that your editor self might scribble in the margins while going through your manuscript in a round of rewriting. (Your rewriter self would be coming along behind, struggling to make fixes.)

I'm sure other writers and editors would have many suggestions to add to this list, but one hundred should be enough to make the point about the breadth and *totality* of concerns that should come under scrutiny as you rewrite.

SMALL (NEEDS SIMPLE FIX)

1. Wrong word?
2. Awkward?
3. Better way to phrase this?
4. Better description?
5. Verbose—needs trimming.
6. Fuzzy—sharpen focus.
7. Spelling okay?
8. Grammar okay?
9. Punctuation okay? Too many commas?
10. Pronoun disagreement causing confusion.
11. Italicize? Underline?
12. More paragraphing? Less?
13. More specific? Less specific?

14. Weak or unclear transition.
15. Unfamiliar reference.
16. Redundant?
17. Irrelevant?
18. Rambling—get back on track.
19. Delete jargon.
20. Delete slang.
21. Delete cliché.
22. Emphasis misplaced?
23. The right adjective? Too many adjectives?
24. This is okay but cut-able.
25. Writing sounds amateurish—work on it.

MEDIUM (NEEDS THOUGHT)

26. Have I said what I'm trying to say?
27. Is this confusing or just inarticulate?
28. Needs more showing, less telling.
29. Livelier opening would improve this.
30. Trying to go in conflicting directions?
31. Too harsh? Soften?
32. Lazy writing? Think harder about this.
33. Make this more interesting or cut it.
34. Good material but needs more energetic writing.
35. Getting too fancy, giddy, showing off.
36. Feels like something's missing from this.
37. This tangent digressing too far from main line?
38. This tangent contributing enough?
39. Overdoing it? Underdoing it?
40. Emotion is ambiguous.
41. Emotion is excessive—calm down.
42. Voice not sounding consistent.
43. More imagery would improve this.
44. A metaphor or comparison might sharpen this thought.
45. Add sensory detail (sights, smells, sounds, touch).
46. Story starts at right place? Ends at right place?
47. An ending or just a stopping?

YOU DON'T HAVE TO BE FAMOUS

48. Find better way to approach or discuss this.
49. Jarring change in level (candor, disclosure, humor).
50. Said same thing fifteen pages ago.
51. Contradicts or conflicts with something said elsewhere?
52. This story belongs in a different chapter.
53. Too many qualifications and reservations.
54. Heavy-handed—lighten up a little.
55. Don't joke about this—not funny.
56. Funny but could be funnier.
57. Not funny—drop it.
58. Doesn't make sense—clarify.
59. Too complicated—simplify.
60. Hard to believe—be more convincing.
61. Trivial facts obscuring main points.
62. Is the mood right?
63. Sarcastic tone doesn't work.
64. Could I find better details?
65. Questionable taste?
66. These facts need checking/confirming.
67. Is this obvious? (Doesn't need to be said.)
68. Really want to reveal this fact?
69. Evade better or don't evade at all.
70. Use definite, specific, concrete language (Principle #16).
71. Too negative? Tone turning nasty.
72. Too sugary? Excessive euphemizing or whitewashing?
73. Change of pace here could help.
74. Better before I changed it?
75. Liked this yesterday—not today.

LARGE (NEEDS SERIOUS INTERVENTION OR RETHINKING)

76. Point of story unclear—why telling this?
77. Explain motivations better.
78. Too many facts—not enough meanings.
79. Chapter (or book) going off course?
80. Chapter idea just not jelling?
81. Drifting away from purpose of anecdote/chapter/book.

82. Is sequence of chapters and stories working?
83. Dig in memory for more depth.
84. Junk this and restart—need fresh approach.
85. One too many stories on this topic?
86. Too much philosophizing—or too little?
87. Could be easily misconstrued.
88. Find example or anecdote to illustrate this.
89. Interpretation of this event keeps changing.
90. ATIDT-ATIDT ("And then I did this ... and then I did that.")
91. Stay out of this area—too sensitive.
92. Sounds like baloney—do I really mean this?
93. Too self-absorbed? Self-centered? Narcissistic?
94. Boo-hoo (self-pitying).
95. Find better story on same subject?
96. Have I made readers care about this?
97. Have I lost touch with reality?
98. True, or do I just want it to be true?
99. Taking myself too seriously? Delusions of grandeur?
100. Needs better ending.

FOUR PAGES BACK, THREE PAGES FORWARD

I'm such a believer in rewriting that I begin it even before my original rough drafting is done. I try to sustain a constant state of rewriting. In younger days, I tried to finish the rough draft with no looking back, but somewhere along the way, I stopped being able to tolerate all that mess behind me. I needed to be building on something more solid.

It's rare now that I start writing where I left off yesterday. Instead, to get reimmersed, I back up a few pages or maybe all the way to the beginning of a section or chapter. I start by rewriting yesterday's pages as a way of building momentum that will carry over into some new pages today.

Let's say on Day One, I write four pages.

YOU DON'T HAVE TO BE FAMOUS

On Day Two, I go over those pages again and manage to add three more.

On Day Three, I'm hoping to breeze through the first four pages, slow down to do some rewriting with the next three, and maybe add four new ones. This would give me eleven pages.

On Day Four, I might start at a section break, if there is one, ideally around page 7 or 8, and maybe aim to have fifteen pages by the end of the day.

On Day Five, I'll work on those newly added pages and add two more, finishing the rough draft.

On Day Six, I'll start rewriting from the beginning, expecting the early pages to be better than the later pages.

The strategy is to keep strengthening the foundation to support the weight of the new stuff I'm adding every day. I think this makes sense because my mastery of the chapter increases so much between Day One (when I'm flailing in the darkness) and Day Five (by which time I should have an advanced notion of where I'm going).

I don't want to begin revising by turning back to my original start and finding a bunch of clueless pages. If this means I spend a disproportionate amount of time rewriting the early pages, going over them many more times than I go over the later pages, that's fine with me. If big problems are solved in the first half, that means fewer problems in the second half.

I've described this in the context of a chapter, but how about the book as a whole? If you write half of your book without looking back, it's a good bet that those early pages are a distant memory. You've made a lot of decisions since then, and by now those old pages might be obsolete. Should you start looking back and revising now, or should you barrel forward? Wouldn't stopping for extensive revision at this point jeopardize your momentum?

I tend to favor momentum (and dread losing it if I have it), but it depends on your comfort level. If you're a little uncertain about what you're building on and feel a need to firm it up, go back—maybe not all the way to the first page of the book but to a sensible entry point. But if you have a compelling idea of what you want to write next, don't risk losing it. Blaze a new trail.

THINK BIGGER

Rewriting is not just about tinkering, polishing, and catching mistakes. James Joyce did not spend twenty thousand hours writing *Ulysses* or seventeen years writing *Finnegans Wake* just to delete adverbs, correct misspellings, or punch up the prose.

Writing is a process for creating and refining thoughts, and there is no reason for this to end when rewriting begins. Don't limit yourself to working *within* the first draft, work *on top of it*. Use it as a base to build on as you move up to higher levels of discovery and creativity.

So while you're scouring your text for small fixes, don't take your mind off the possibility of making radical, change-everything improvements. You might stumble on new directions, new perspectives, or structural ideas that give you a whole new vision (drop a hyphen into "revision" at the right place and you get "re-vision").

Now is the time to have the courage and energy to embark on big changes even if it means discarding a lot of old work or even putting the whole thing in a drawer and starting something new and better. The new work probably won't be as hard as you expect because you've *already*

YOU DON'T HAVE TO BE FAMOUS

got the idea and a lot of momentum to go with it. And once you see the opportunity to raise the quality level by whole dimensions, you won't be able to resist.

I've described the magic-zone experience in the context of the first draft, but it can happen again in the rewriting, and it can be bigger and better because, having worked through a first draft, you're deeper into the material.

Suddenly you're re-reading something for the twentieth time —something you hadn't thought much about or something you'd found vaguely wrong or unsatisfactory—and that amazing *access* returns.

The clouds part, and the better way is revealed. It's just there, waiting to be found, and it seems easy except you had to make nineteen uneventful passes before finding gold on the twentieth time around. The gold might be just a single word that crystallizes a whole new idea, or it could be a whole new out-of-nowhere idea that causes you to rewrite many pages.

This is the reward for all your grueling effort, and you don't have to be working on James Joyce's level to be thrilled by it. Thank the rewriting process for getting you to this place.

WHEN DOES REWRITING END?

Rewriting always goes on longer than you expect, and there may be false endings. You'll pronounce the draft complete, but the next morning, you're working on it again. Much as you want to be done, you'll find that you are magnetically pulled back to your desk to do more rewriting. It's astonishing how many times you can go over the same writing and keep finding things to improve, and not just small things.

A very sophisticated writing tip—often suggested as a last thing to do before declaring a writing project finished—is to go through everything and *delete* any fancy flourishes or grand flights of language. You take secret pride in these gems as your *showpiece* achievements, but in truth, they are *show off* achievements. It's hard to part with them—Isaac Bashevis Singer called it "killing your babies"—but the heartless truth is that a day later, if you even remember what you cut, you'll be glad it's gone.

At some point, external reality—such as constraints on your time—might push you to declare that rewriting has gone on long enough. But if you have a choice, keep rewriting until you absolutely can't find anything else to change.

And then you're done. It's over.

Two matters remain. One is deciding exactly what you're going to do with that manuscript, since the range of private publishing options is extensive. The other is preparing yourself for reader reaction.

"NOT GOOD ENOUGH"

This is a special section devoted to my favorite criticism.

Earlier I mentioned one of my college creative writing teachers, Nancy Packer (who would write, "What's at stake here?" in the margins of student short stories). Something else she scrawled in margins was, "NOT GOOD ENOUGH."

I think it is now politically incorrect to swing a wrecking ball of this power against the sensitive psyche of a writing student, and I recall being devastated and outraged when I found those words next to some show-off undergraduate paragraphs I'd crafted, taking pride in what I thought was their likelihood of literary immortality. *Not good enough?* What kind of constructive criticism is this? This is not helpful, I fumed. This is gratuitously brutal.

But as I calmed down, I realized she was right. In fact, her diagnosis was spot-on perfect. There was nothing *wrong* with what I'd written, it just wasn't good enough. This particular moment in the short story required something really good instead of something really mediocre.

This wasn't an error that could be fixed with pencil editing, and there was no point describing *why* it wasn't good enough, it just wasn't. And the solution was obvious: WRITE SOMETHING BETTER.

As I think back on this experience, I enjoy Mrs. Packer's rough candor, but I'm also flattered that she didn't tell me *how* to write something better. I think her message was, "I would never write 'NOT GOOD ENOUGH' on your story if I didn't think you were capable of writing something better. You don't need me to tell you how—you'll solve that on your own, and that's the way it should be."

From that point on, the person who wrote "NOT GOOD ENOUGH" in my margins was me, and the person who took responsibility for writing something better was me. It was a big step forward in my maturity as a writer.

YOU'RE FINISHED, NOW WHAT?

You're done. You have made the long crawl across the burning desert and crossed the finish line. Is it time to celebrate? I don't see why not. But when your head clears tomorrow, there will be things to think about.

You'll have to decide—if you haven't already—what physical form your book will take. I'll suggest some options momentarily. Before that, let's talk about preparing yourself emotionally.

First, don't be surprised if, as you finish writing, you realize you've become attached to the book and don't want to let it go. Rewriting, which had become grueling, then became addicting. Even though you know in your heart that you're done, you'd like to run through the final draft one more time—it might need a few more little edits. You realize that you've developed a close *relationship* with the book. You sense correctly that releasing it to the world will break the bubble of that relationship, forever changing its private nature.

Second, you should prepare yourself to deal with reader reaction.

BRACE FOR UNPREDICTABLE READER REACTIONS

Lawyers say you can never know what a jury will decide. Movie producers know you can't predict how audiences will respond to a new movie (it's a Hollywood adage that "Nobody knows nothing" about what audiences will like). The only thing that makes reaction to your book a little more predictable than juries and movies is that your audience of family and friends is presumably looking forward to your book, and they're disposed to like it, unless you shock or alienate them. If you're lucky, everyone will love the book and tell you so emphatically. But don't count on that.

The reaction that will throw you off balance is a *small* reaction, meaning minimal feedback beyond a few pleasant compliments. Some people will never say anything, not realizing you were holding your breath, waiting for their reaction. Others will misplace the book and think nothing of it. Some will mean to read it but never get around to it. But even people who do read it might be silent or nearly silent, and this dismays you.

Let me suggest an explanation.

People who work in show business know that a performer—or anyone who faces an audience of any kind—takes a terrible risk going out on the stage. You are exposing yourself to potentially humiliating judgment. The stakes, to you, are very high, and you are very vulnerable.

When you come offstage, you require immediate assurance that your gamble in the spotlight has paid off with spectacular success. Not just a little assurance, you want a *mountain* of it. Show business people understand this and generously heap on the congratulations and flattery.

This might seem absurdly egotistical to you now, but wait until you bring out your book. You have poured your heart and soul into it. You have thrown open your life and invited readers to measure not only your writing skill but the worth of your existence.

The very *least* you want is for the book to be taken seriously. You would obviously prefer acclaim and approval, but even a mixed reaction is better than a big ho hum. Yet many people—the vast majority who've never written a book or faced an audience—don't understand the magnitude of your emotional investment or the nature of your need.

Someone says, "Hey, that was pretty good" or "I haven't gotten around to reading it yet, but I'm looking forward to it," and you feel as if a red-hot spear has pierced your heart. You translate these phrases as "That was the most atrocious piece of garbage I've ever seen" and "I would languish for twenty years in a fetid, vermin-infested dungeon before I would read a single word of that drivel."

But this is *not* what they mean to say. What's really happening is that people don't know how to cope with your sudden emergence as a book writer. They are impressed but uncertain about how to express it. They don't want to overdo it or look unsophisticated, going gaga just because someone they know wrote a book.

Given the lack of evidence to the contrary, you start wondering if you've failed. But then a year goes by, and you find yourself in a casual conversation with a friend who says something like, "I've been thinking about that

YOU DON'T HAVE TO BE FAMOUS

autobiography you wrote. I'd give anything if I could ever write something that great."

"Great?" you say. "I thought you hated it."

"Hated it? Why would you ever think that?"

So for your own emotional survival, be ready to interpret a low-key reaction to your book *not* as a judgment on its quality but as a reflection of your readers' inexpressiveness. Let some time pass before you make a serious assessment of how readers really felt about it.

All of this goes double when it comes to your children. If there is anyone whose reaction is especially important to you, it is theirs. You may have written the book for them; you may have been motivated all along by anticipation of the moment when you would present it to them.

Perhaps they will appreciate this, but maybe they won't. You should be prepared for the latter. They're just not interested. Maybe they thumb though it, looking for stories about themselves and then put it aside. For any number of reasons from shallow to deep, that is the extent of their demonstrated interest and appreciation. This happens. All you can do is hope they'll become interested later, or perhaps that *their* children will be a more interested audience.

There is one aggressive measure you can take to try to prevent a painfully insufficient reaction when you release your book to the world: Throw yourself a book party. (Even better, get someone else to throw it for you.)

Invite all your intended readers. Make it an event, festive and good-humored, calculated to win their hearts and minds. Decorate the room with enlarged nostalgic photos of you and each guest in your younger days—reminding them of the role they played in your life story.

Autograph each book with a nice, personal inscription and hand out copies individually as your guests head for the door (*do not* distribute copies until the party is ending—you don't want a bunch of people sitting around reading in dead silence).

Before it's time to go, stand up and make a few modest remarks about how much the book means to you and how you hope it's meaningful to them. No doubt this is shameless self-promotion, but it also sends an important message: *This book is big to me, don't ignore it*. A book party like this would not be everyone's cup of tea, but if this fits your personality, go for it.

One more thought about reader reaction. We go into book writing and other creative projects thinking—with absolutely no logical reason—that everyone will love the result. But this *never* happens. In the history of literature, no one has written anything that's been greeted with 100 percent enthusiasm. It is an inflexible rule of life that *you can't please everybody*. No matter how hard you try or how far you bend over backwards, there will always be displeased readers. They'll be hurt or offended for a million different reasons. They'll be especially displeased because you said more about someone else than you said about them, or because you failed to shower them with effusive tributes or identify them as the most significant person in your life.

You might anticipate some of these feelings early in the writing process and take acceptable measures—if you've mentioned three of four cousins, it might be kind to find a way of mentioning the fourth—but trying to cater to everyone is hopeless, and it will undermine the integrity and purpose of the book. So don't even try.

Just hope the unhappy readers keep it to themselves so you don't have to contend with it.

In the end, you cannot measure the value of the book by the way readers react to it. The reaction is never as much as you want, and it may be a lot *less* than you want, so keep it in its proper perspective, which is secondary.

What does count is how *you* feel—how fulfilled you are by having met the challenge and completed the effort of writing your first book, how much you've learned from telling your story, and how much you sincerely meant to leave something of value for those who live on, even if they don't realize right away what a wonderful gift you've given them. If you feel good about it, it's an achievement to enjoy wholeheartedly, even if the enjoyment is more solitary than you had in mind. Now let's think about what you do with your manuscript.

NO-TECH AND LOW-TECH PUBLISHING OPTIONS

For several years, I resisted digital photography, thinking it would be an exhausting challenge—it turned out to be easy and fun. I suspect most publishing options are not too difficult, though some professional desktop publishing programs require some training, and some aspects of self-publishing require extended attention to logistics and details.

Another factor is cost. You can spend just about *any* amount, small or large.

Another factor is glitz, by which I mean the physical and aesthetic attractiveness of the physical book.

You can have it professionally printed and bound in a hard cover with a photo of yourself on the jacket, and it will look like a bookstore-quality book. Or it can look like a report you did in high school. Or it can be a computer file you distribute by e-mail. Or it can be any of many variations in between.

The low end of the technology, cost, and glitz scales would be a book written in quill and ink with pages bound by a ribbon or piece of string. This model sufficed for many centuries. It still works, and it makes a statement about how you feel about the fancy modern way of doing things.

A step up would be a computer-printed manuscript with copies made by printer or photocopier. Bind it in a simple folder from Staples. Plastic coil or comb bindings (similar to loose-leaf binding) are a little nicer, but you'll need to buy or borrow a hole-punching and binding machine.

The personal autobiographies I've seen go no farther than this. One friend sent around a 155-page autobiography on an Adobe computer file. It was my option to print it out or read it on the monitor screen. I read it on the screen.

At this level, the production effort and cost are only slightly above nil. The glitz is zero, but the final product is unpretentious and serviceable and might be ideally suited to your temperament and ambition for the book. Nothing about it distracts in any way from the central ingredient, which is your telling of your story. No one will accuse you of putting on author airs or living a literary fantasy.

You can modify this solution for the better by inserting even a modest assortment of photos and perhaps copies of old documents such as letters, diplomas, report cards, crayon drawings (briefly borrowed from the refrigerator door), or scrapbook items from cocktail napkins to old ID cards to who-knows-what-else you'll find when you start searching around in old cartons and desk drawers. Photos, of course, are best.

When my son was twelve years old, he accepted an invitation to a baseball game which turned out to be a once-in-a-lifetime event for a sports fan, a perfect game pitched by David Wells of the New York Yankees. My son came home with his ticket stub and photos of himself at the game with his best friend, and later we accumulated a collection of newspaper clippings and other documents related to the game. I mention this as an example of the kind of material that would make for a lively collage in an autobiography—my son's or even mine.

The low-tech way to present photos and documents is to make a page layout (adding scissored-out text if you want to integrate text and pictures), taping your photos to a blank page and photocopying them, later inserting the photo pages into your text. Photocopying pages with color costs a lot more than black-and-white but probably less than a dollar per page (multiplied by the number of books, of course). You can decide whether including a dozen or a half-dozen color pages is worth the price.

If you are familiar with desktop publishing, you can probably go the do-it-yourself route and create something quite impressive. If not, I suggest that you consider options you might discover browsing photography Web sites or local print shops. Look under "Printers" in a yellow pages directory and start making calls. I suggest trying FedEx Kinko's—even if there is no Kinko's close by, you can send your manuscript as an e-mail attachment or mail it on a CD.

I asked several local print shops, including Kinko's, how much it would cost to print fifty copies of a 120-page manuscript plus a half-dozen pages with color pictures, single-sided pages bound with comb binders. The estimates were in the high hundreds, none reaching a thousand dollars. Adding hard-cover glue binding instead of a comb binding would double the price. The prices in your local stores will surely be different; do some comparison shopping and don't forget to try for a discount.

PRINT-ON-DEMAND SELF-PUBLISHING

This is a new world and a big step upward from the do-it-yourself approach, although the term *do-it-yourself* continues to be applied—misleadingly, I think, since both involve hiring professionals.

There are two higher levels of self-publishing, each resulting in a book that seems to be of bookstore quality, although I tend to be old-fashioned and presume that full-fledged traditional publishers will always produce a better book. The catch, of course, is that traditional publishers will probably not publish your book, and if you're footing the bill yourself, cheap might be good.

Another key virtue of the two self-publishing options is that they allow you to feasibly print only a small number of books (even a single copy) using technology known as print-on-demand. This, of course, is ideal for a private autobiography.

The print-on-demand (POD) model emerged in the mid-1990s and is a great improvement on the old "vanity" method of self-publishing, which was low on services to the author but high on charges.

Think of print-on-demand as a magnified version of sending a document from your computer to your printer and printing copies one at a time. The difference is that

YOU DON'T HAVE TO BE FAMOUS

POD uses bigger, faster printers and large servers that can store not only your text but everything else, including the book's jacket.

One of the two self-publishing options is what I would call "manage it yourself," in which you hire professionals for specific functions but oversee the whole, complex process on your own. This demands a high commitment of supervisory effort, time, learning, and possibly expense and seems to create a high probability of first-timer mistakes.

Having paid for the book's production, you maintain full ownership of the book, and this is good if you are highly enterprising and think you can make money selling it yourself (e.g., you are a lecturer and believe you can get audiences excited enough to buy your book on the way out) or if you believe that once your book is in print, it will be discovered and snapped up by big publishers who will pay you handsomely for it. There are a few cases of this happening, but I must now revert to the party-pooper spirit of my first chapter and urge you to reject fantasies of book-related celebrity and profit, especially if they threaten your bank account as well as your emotions.

The second option is, I think, more attractive. It is usually called "supported self-publishing," meaning that you turn your book over to a company that supports you by doing most of the work, providing the book-production expertise, and offering services (for which you pay extra) such as editing, book design, and jacket design.

There are dozens of companies that do this, but the big names are AuthorHouse, iUniverse, Lulu, and Xlibris (all have easy-to-find Web sites). They offer bare bones packages in the hundreds of dollars, but be prepared to go into the low thousands as you elect different options. The good news is that if you're not selling your book, you won't need to pay a nickel for marketing, publicity, distribution, or book-warehousing services.

This route is considered do-it-yourself, but in fact there's very little to do yourself. All you have to do is prepare your manuscript, approve the book's design and jacket, make a few other decisions, and place your order. The self-publishing company, with its streamlined processes and technology, does the rest. You sit back and wait for a few weeks or months until the books arrive.

The argument for spending more than minimal money on producing your book is that you've put blood, sweat, and tears into writing it, and you might not be doing yourself justice if you take an overly humble approach to presenting it. So investigate different options and don't shortchange yourself. I hate to play the "on the other hand" game, but I feel a need to jump in here immediately with a word of caution: I've heard stories of runaway fees that raise the cost of self-publishing far beyond what the author expected. So rather than shortchanging yourself, you might be making yourself a victim—a thought that suggests rethinking more modest options that might be perfectly satisfactory to your family and friends.

Whatever level you choose, if you need help or advice, you should definitely seek it. Professionals are available to help you with just about every step in the process.

You should definitely consider a copy editor or proofreader because writing mistakes and small errors like typos and misspellings will mar your long-term satisfaction with the finished book. Here again, there are consumer stories of incompetence and even scams, so don't hire just anyone. Check out references and look for trustworthy word-of-mouth recommendations.

If your photographs are amateurish or damaged, find professionals who can clean or restore them, crop them, or reshoot them. You should definitely include a high-quality current photo of yourself.

If Cost Is No Object

A speechwriting client of mine was nearing the end of his legendary corporate career and turned his attention to a lifelong ambition: He wanted to write a book. He and I had discussed it many times, starting in the early 1990s, but it seemed unlikely that the book he had in mind (built around his speeches) would be marketable enough to attract traditional publishers.

But then technology changed the book business, and, by chance, he met the president of a small publishing house in California, and she connected him to the right writer to adapt his speeches to book form. He hired them to write and publish the book he always wanted. Both had good track records and did a good job for him, but I should point out that given his personal wealth, the risk was negligible; the worst possible financial loss would have been no more than a drop in the bucket.

Given the small risk and high reward, he spared no expense. The book was meticulously produced with a beautiful jacket (his photograph, taken by one of the world's top portrait photographers, Annie Leibovitz) and a photo section. He had ten thousand copies printed and went into his pocket to buy advertising in major publications. He gave many of the books away as gifts but sold a lot of them, too, and actually made a small profit.

There was no problem with an inadequate reader reaction. He mailed copies of the book to a long list of contacts. They replied with lavish praise. He was widely saluted. Friends gave him parties. He was invited to give speeches. Instead of fading out at the end of his career, his star shined brighter than ever.

The book's success was gratifying, but what was most important was that he achieved his dream of creating a tangible book that he could hold in his hand and see on his living room shelf. He presented the first copy to his wife at a party celebrating their fiftieth wedding anniversary. His family was deeply moved.

Few of us have the resources to fly first class to this degree, but learn from his example. This is your life story, your one-and-only autobiography, the chosen time to create and leave your record. Give serious thought to doing it right.

ADDING AUDIO AND VIDEO

Nothing beats the printed word for a detailed and substantive record of your life, but you can add a dimension of value by supplementing what you've written with audio or video.

I'm aware that some people would prefer to skip the writing altogether and go right to the audio/video. That's a very different choice, and if you have read this book up to this point, it's probably not *your* choice. On the other hand, you shouldn't be phobic or old-fashioned about audio or video.

I had two wonderful and colorful grandfathers who died when I was seven and seventeen years old. I would be thrilled to be able to hear their voices again or to see them alive on videotape.

Even better—and of course only a fantasy at this point—how about audio or videotape monologues *by them addressed to me*, talking about their lives, their thoughts, their hopes, and their feelings for me.

YOU DON'T HAVE TO BE FAMOUS

This sort of message is something you could leave for *your* grandchildren. You could write it out in advance or just sit down and talk, recording it on audiotape or a CD (the CD has a longer life expectancy).

You could also buy a small recording device and carry it around, describing your life and recording your thoughts for posterity. You could do something similar on video-tape. You could interview yourself, mounting the camera on a tripod, or you could ask a friend to operate the camera and interview you. You could conduct videotaped guided tours of your home or neighborhood. You could talk about old times using photos as illustration.

Three quick generalizations about audio or video:

★ We are a nation of sophisticated viewers, which means that we quickly tire of amateur-ish production, even by loved ones. Therefore, editing is indispensable—unedited audio or video is unbearably boring, something you do not want to inflict on future generations. This means you must acquire equipment and learn how to use it, or get someone to do it for you.

★ Detailed preparation always enhances the fi-nal product. Have a written script or at least a thought-out plan about what you're going to say. But then be open to the spontaneous and unexpected: If a wonderful home movie breaks out before your eyes, grab it and work it into your plan. The plan is there to assure quality, not to prevent quality.

★ If you're not familiar with camera and audio equipment, you might be able to find someone in your family to help out, but, even better, hire a professional. Quality counts—this is for posterity.

If you are really ambitious, you can make a full-fledged autobiographical video, a profile of yourself. If this interests you, read the short appendix I've added at the end of this book, titled Profiling Yourself on Video.

AFTERWORD:
MY NOT-YET-WRITTEN
AUTOBIOGRAPHY

I've always thought of autobiography writing as an ideal retirement activity. The main reason I haven't written my own story yet is that I haven't retired.

In the world of a freelance writer, you take jobs as they come to you. When they stop coming, you have time to write what you want. With no deadlines or clamoring clients, you can relax and make it a labor of love. Possibly, by the time you read this book, I'll be at work on my life story.

A second reason why I've kept the autobiography on hold is that from the moment *this* book came into my mind, I assumed that writing it would help clarify ideas and build motivation to write my autobiography. And it has.

I've created the *Notes* file, which, for me, is the initial step in any writing project. In addition to collecting a scattering of random notes, I've begun to see the light on how I'll structure the book, and I've solved the big problem of where I'll start.

The day my wife and two kids and I moved into our current home, my daughter, who was just a few days short of five years old, was exploring her new backyard. It was daytime, but, for reasons long forgotten, she was wearing an outfit that would have made more sense if she'd escaped from the house during a fire in the night: a nightgown and a pair of seemingly enormous adult tennis shoes. She was at the bottom of a slope, taking big climbing steps uphill while conducting an excited monologue about the trees, rocks, and squirrels that caught her interest.

Watching her, the thought that entered my mind was: I want this to be the last image to go through my mind before I die. I didn't mean this in a morbid sense, far from it—I would be going out with one of the happiest images of my life.

But what about her twin brother? I had no corresponding image of him, and this was a glaring deficiency until, when he was about seven, I watched him in a wild, screaming game of tag with friends in the local school yard. They frolicked like puppies, chasing each other in circles, giggling riotously, falling down and bouncing up, eager to play. This gave me another richly happy image.

I'm going to start my book with these two images.

The opening chapter will cover the kids' births and early childhoods and then lead to the present as I describe the current state of my life and my goals in writing my autobiography. The narrative perspective throughout the book will be based in the present but looking back.

I'll return to the kids' stories later. The second chapter might begin with an overview of my family—not just kids but aunts and uncles, cousins, everybody. I might also report on long-term friends. Having surveyed the present,

YOU DON'T HAVE TO BE FAMOUS

I would then turn back to the chronological beginning I sketched out in chapter four—about my diverse family background, my parents, and their marriage. This chapter might end with my birth, but who knows, I might not be born for a few more chapters.

The book's structure will be based on key people in different periods of my life, in a roughly chronological order. Each chapter will begin with reflections on a particular period, and then I'll dive into it, concentrating on the people I remember from that time and letting memory reach back for details and anecdotes. The history of those periods will provide background—Vietnam, Watergate, the Carter and Reagan years, the prosperity of the 1990s, 9/11 and the emergence of anti-American terrorism in 2001. I'll also have to peek into old cartons and boxes to assess what I have in the way of photos and documents. This should produce some portraits and good scenes, and I'm sure it will ripple out to include memories of more people and more scenes. A chapter might consist of four or five separate stories or profiles of several different characters.

I think it will be easier to remember people than periods ("Hmmm, what did I do in my early thirties?" or "What did I do in 1997?"). Periods might be indistinct, but people memories come back sharply. I cannot guess the length or number of chapters, but I won't be surprised if I end up with a long first draft. The weaker recollections will bite the dust in the rewriting phase.

I'm looking forward to starting my life story, and I hope you feel the same way.

Chapter one of this book began, "You should do it."

Let me amend that: *We should do it.*

Let's begin without delay.

APPENDIX:
PROFILING YOURSELF
ON VIDEO

By "profiling" yourself I mean creating a TV-newsmag-azine-style video piece about your life. It can be any length—I would suggest ten minutes, but it can be a lot more or less, depending on the quality and nature of your material. You can be its narrator or someone else can read the voice-over narration, which you will write as part of a video script.

Professional video writers usually structure their scripts around the best available visuals, so your first step would be collecting all the still photos, old home movies and videos, or new shot scenes that you will want to use. If possible, shoot scenes of yourself at your birthplace, in your home, interacting with your family and best friends, fishing, hiking, sailing, working, whatever.

Then write a script indicating how the visuals will be used, either as audio-video scenes in which you hear *and* see yourself talking or (if you have editing capability) as "B-roll." In the early days of film, there was only a single roll of film, but as projection became more sophisticated, it was possible to run numerous rolls simultaneously, switching between them. In TV production, the A-roll would usually mean the significant audio while the B-roll would be illustrative video. So you might see the president on camera declaring war—that's the A-roll—and then as the president's audio continues, you would see shots of troops, tanks, and bombers—that's the B-roll. Production people would say the military video was running "under" the continuing presidential narration. Short excerpts of narration are called "sound bites." A head-and-shoulders shot of someone speaking is called a "talking head."

Professionals write video scripts using two parallel vertical columns—the column on the right is the audio (on-camera and voice-over narration or transcribed sound bites or natural sound such as a band playing) while the column on the left indicates matching visuals.

A frustration for print writers trying video production for the first time is that you always have to "cover" whatever's being said with pictures of something, and this means your narration as well as your sound bites have to be far more succinct than you're used to.

The way to make a longer "talking head" tolerable is to run B-roll video as the speaker's voice continues. Thus, we might see you sitting on a living room chair and talking for ten seconds or so about how important travel has been in your life; then, still hearing your voice, we would see B-roll video or still photos taken during your favorite trips. The more interesting the B-roll, the longer you can go with the sound bite. It also helps to create variety on the audio side, mixing in different voices, perhaps alternating between yourself and a narrator or voices of people you interview.

When interviewing people, sit them down in undistracting conditions (*not* in the kitchen with family members standing around watching and kids chasing each other through the room). You should ask questions from off camera while the camera stays on their faces to record their answers, which you will later edit. You can operate the camera, or have someone else operate it, or mount it on a tripod and let it operate itself—the most comfortable interviewing will come when the interviewee talks to you eye to eye instead of you with a lens blocking your face.

Of course, you could hire a professional to make this videotape for you. I have a friend who is a former network producer and now owns his own production company. He showed me a video tribute he made to the deceased wife of a (very affluent) client. The production was top quality and the client was so thrilled that he didn't flinch at the bill, $165,000. I think you can find a professional who will do a satisfactory job for much, much less.

If you want to make the video yourself, plan it carefully in advance. Make a chart showing what the audio and video will be at every point in the tape. Have a list of prepared questions for your interviews and be clear in your mind exactly what you're after. You don't want to get to the editing stage and say, "I did this interview just to get the dog story but totally forgot to ask about the dog." However, if an interview takes off on a different direction, and it's good, stay with it—but remember to come back and get the dog story before you wrap up.

As preparation for interviewing anyone on camera, chat with them off camera. Find out what they've got to say and what you want to hear—this will allow you

YOU DON'T HAVE TO BE FAMOUS

to go right to the main point when you interview them, without excessive circling in.

Get a sense of how they'll answer various questions and how well they'll tell particular stories. Some people are camera shy and get very nervous when a camera is on them, and you'll have to work hard to put them at ease. Sometimes, you'll see that they're incapable of performing the way you want, but other times, with some encouragement and a few extra "takes," they'll be better than expected. Sometimes it's good to "waste" a few questions at the start—you probably won't use their answers, but this gives them a minute or two to find their voice and relax as much as they can.

Try to put them in an upbeat mood before you start. A friend who produces documentary films tells of working with a distinguished author who often narrates films and videos. Before recording voice-overs, they turn on loud 1960s Chubby Checker music and dance "The Twist" for a minute or two, completely uninhibited and silly. Then, considerably loosened up, they begin recording.

Your interviewees will be more comfortable if you give them a general idea of the questions you'll be asking. But don't put words into their mouths, and don't give them time to compose and memorize answers, which will come out stiffly.

When you conduct the interviews, be relaxed but serious, not allowing your session to turn giddy. Keep eye contact with your interviewees and show them that you are paying attention to what they're saying (not fiddling with the camera or studying your notes to find your next question).

If they give an especially good answer or tell an especially good story (encourage storytelling), but something goes wrong—a sneeze, a ringing phone, a freeze up or stumble or senior moment—go back to the beginning of the question or story and try it again. Do several "takes" if necessary, but don't exhaust interviewees by making them do everything again.

In my view, the video should supplement or complement your written autobiography, and the two should be kept together. But a question that puzzles me is how do you keep the tape or disk from becoming physically—and permanently—separated from the printed book?

My best thought is adding a pocket or envelope to the book and keeping the video inside it. The problem is that we know that in almost every household, things that are not nailed down inevitably migrate to other places, drawers or shelves where they are overlooked or lost or accidentally thrown away. I simply don't have an answer for this other than being vigilant and perhaps begging people to remember to put the CD back inside the book. Ideally, I would like to link the video to the book using a heavy chain and a big padlock and then throwing away the key.

Finally, let's discuss the important issue of length, because there are two different ways to approach your video.

One is the professional style, which I've been describing. Professional doctrine is that everything must be ultra short. The average sound bite on network TV news is nine seconds long, which might be the length of a single sentence. American viewers are conditioned to fast-changing activity in both audio and video. Doctrine says viewers will go berserk with impatience if forced to pay attention to a thirty-second sound bite.

In TV production, length is always a tug-of-war between producers who want everything short to create a feeling of energy and writers who battle to make things longer because they love the good content and will sacrifice some energy to preserve it. Usually the producers win, and the writers are frustrated because only the tip of the iceberg made it into the final piece.

The other approach is what I respectfully call amateur video. Throw away the professional doctrine. This is your life, and to you, it is the most interesting story in the world, so the normal rules are suspended. Compressing everything into speedy little bites is the opposite of what you want—you want the fullness, the naturalness, the spontaneity, the unedited truth told in a way that people will always treasure and enjoy (even if they would be bored senseless by a similar piece about someone else's life).

A friend who read an early version of this appendix reminded me to praise the virtues of the amateur approach and make sure people understand that they don't have to follow the professional way if their "make it up as you go along" way is better.

"I have a video of my grandmother and about eight of her twelve siblings sitting around talking in front of a camera about their days growing up in a farmhouse without running water," she wrote.

"People are talking over each other, there is rambling, and sometimes it's hard to follow. But it's still great. If they had tried to take turns, organize a script, they would have never made the video. ... It's fine to tell people the 'right' way to do it, but make sure that you leave people the option of just winging it and doing an unprofessional job. That is one of the only videos my grandpa and the rest of my family have of my grandmother, and it would have been a shame to lose something so meaningful because they didn't feel like they could do it professionally."

INDEX